THE CORCORAN GALLERY OF ART

THE FORTY-FIFTH BIENNIAL

The Corcoran Collects, 1907–1998

INTRODUCTION *by David C. Levy*
FOREWORD *by Jack Cowart*
ESSAYS *by Linda Simmons, Terrie Sultan*

THE CORCORAN GALLERY OF ART, WASHINGTON DC

This catalogue was published on the occasion of the exhibition *The Forty-fifth Biennial: The Corcoran Collects, 1907-1998*, organized by the Corcoran Gallery of Art, Washington, DC.

This exhibition was organized at the Corcoran Gallery of Art by Jack Cowart, Deputy Director and Chief Curator, Linda Simmons, Curator of American Art and Research, and Terrie Sultan, Curator of Contemporary Art.

The Forty-fifth Biennial: The Corcoran Collects, 1907-1998 is underwritten by the Anna E. Clark Fund. The catalogue accompanying this exhibition is supported by the Corcoran's Andrew W. Mellon Art Publications and Research Fund and the Kathrine Dulin Folger Fund.

Introduction: David C. Levy
Foreword: Jack Cowart
Essayists: Linda Simmons, Terrie Sultan
Project Manager: Paige Turner
Editors: Nancy Eickel, Lee A. Vedder

ISBN 088675–056–3
ISSN 8756–4777

Published in 1998 by the Corcoran Gallery of Art, 500 Seventeenth Street NW, Washington, DC 20006

This catalogue was designed by Lisa Ratkus, the Corcoran Gallery of Art, and typeset in Adobe Caslon and Copperplate. 2,000 copies were printed on Potlatch McCoy by Chroma Graphics, Inc., Largo, MD.
Photography by Peter Harholdt except for: Corcoran staff photographer, p. 19, p. 39, p. 40 (top), p. 42, p. 54, p. 63, p. 112 (top), p. 123; Oren Slor, p. 58; Sarah Wells, p. 75 (bottom); Sue Tallon, p. 83; Jennifer Kotter, p. 85; John Bessler, p. 87.

Cover: Edward Hopper, *Ground Swell*, 1939, Museum Purchase, William A. Clark Fund.

TABLE OF CONTENTS

INTRODUCTION

David C. Levy, President and Director

At the beginning of this century, biennial and other juried exhibitions in American museums were our version of the French and English academic salons. Absent today's sophisticated communications media, high-quality reproduction techniques, the art press, and the international art market that developed by mid-century, Biennials at this museum, the triennial Carnegie International in Pittsburgh or, later on, the Whitney Biennial in New York (to name a few) became principal forums in which the latest ideas in painting and sculpture could be presented, examined, and debated.

Today, some 90 years after the Corcoran mounted its first Biennial, we have to ask whether the impact of such exhibitions has been so drastically altered by the changed environment in which they take place as to make them anachronistic. Posing this question by no means suggests that we have reached such a conclusion, but it is certainly reflective of the fact that the question has hung heavily over us as we have planned Biennials throughout the 1990s. Why and how, we wonder, does our Biennial (or any other for that matter) differ from the many shows in American museums selected by curators and/or juries who are interested in exploring the contemporary art scene?

Clearly, one of the best ways to explore this question is to examine present practice in light of past experience. The 90-year succession of Corcoran Biennials, their impact on our museum and their effect on the art world as a whole, provides a significant body of data upon which we can begin to consider the changing nature and importance of this show.

Certainly, the evidence demonstrates that the Corcoran's collection has consistently benefited from the acquisition of Biennial works. Perhaps more importantly, many of its key holdings in 20th-century American art would not have been acquired were it not for Biennial purchases. So it is probably fair to say that the Biennial has been and remains an important means through which this particular museum has renewed itself. However the larger questions—of the importance of such exhibitions today or of their potential contributions to the cultural establishment in the coming century—remain complex and problematic.

A good argument might be made that the work of contemporary artists, as well as critical scholarship in this field, are now so accessible as to make Grand Exhibitions with all the trappings of a biennial not only a thing of the past but an institutional conceit. Yet, experience suggests that despite an uneven and sometimes controversial history, such exhibits (particularly at this museum) have played a progressive and salutary role.

As the century ends, we mount this "retrospective" Biennial exhibition to pose and to focus such questions for ourselves as well as for the museum world, the critical community, and the public. We hope the exercise will help us to gain new insight into our own history and will help all of us to understand the ways in which we can continue, in William Wilson Corcoran's words, to "encourage the American genius" as we enter the new millennium.

We are deeply indebted to Deputy Director and Chief Curator, Jack Cowart, for his vision and leadership in the realization of this publication. We also thank the exhibition's curators, Linda Crocker Simmons and Terrie Sultan. Additional thanks go to Assistant Curators of Exhibitions, Paige Turner and Laura Coyle, Archivist Marisa Keller, and Graphic Design Director, Lisa Ratkus, for their roles in the preparation, editing, and design of this publication. Finally, we are pleased, once again, to acknowledge, with deep gratitude, the Anna E. Clark Fund, the Kathrine Dulin Folger Fund, and the Andrew W. Mellon Art Publications and Research Fund of the Corcoran Gallery for their generous support of this publication and of the *The Forty-fifth Biennial: The Corcoran Collects, 1907–1998.*

— D.C.L.

THE CORCORAN BIENNIAL DURING THE TWENTIETH CENTURY: RETRO OR RADAR?

Jack Cowart, Deputy Director and Chief Curator

This 1998 Biennial intentionally differs from all other Corcoran Biennials. For this, the 45th Biennial, we have decided to analyze the preceding forty-four Biennials of this century by displaying more than 130 of our acquisitions from these exhibitions. By looking back over this visual panorama, we may see where we have been, where we might have gone, and all that we have done. We may also find inspiration to apply towards our Biennials for the coming century and new millennium.

It is endlessly fashionable and seductive to review past events and decisions, judging them with the false superiority gained from 20/20 hindsight. Patterns emerge, of course, but they are mostly visible at a distance that can both clarify and distort. To attempt to understand and learn from the past, we have developed that peculiar intellectual and analytical process called History. This liberal art comprises an ever-shifting, complex blend of elements that include the studies of social, political, religious, military, economic, environmental, and art histories. To make this analysis even more interesting, value systems change over time. Things deemed significant to one generation are perhaps not important to either preceding or subsequent generations.

THE CONTEXT

The Corcoran Biennial and its relevance have been variously affected by all these histories during the last century. Our Biennial, founded in 1907, evolved as one of the earliest and most progressive of our nation's biennial exhibitions. In the first decade of the twentieth century, the American museum system was still in its relative youth. Frequently run by dedicated committees of civilian or artist volunteers, the nation's museums, galleries, and art associations were just beginning to become professional organizations. Contemporary artists and their art were slowly becoming publicly visible, as cultural mass communication was itself in its own infancy.

WILLIAM MERRITT
CHASE (1849–1916)

William Andrews Clark,
c. 1915

Oil on canvas
Gift of William Andrews
Clark
THE 6TH BIENNIAL

Over the last nine decades, the Corcoran Biennial has not been one unchanging, programmatic "thing." It always has had, however, a central ideal and a number of related intentions. Its ideal, like that of the Corcoran's institutional mission, has been to focus on creativity and to support and encourage American genius in the arts. The intention of the exhibition's founders was to promote public interest in the new facilities of the privately funded Corcoran Gallery and School of Art. The founders also aspired to benefit the participating painters. Further, the Biennial was designed to encourage artistic vitality as well as our national pride. Finally, by showing paintings not previously seen in Washington, the organizers hoped to instruct both art lovers and the general public.

The independent Corcoran was the only logical place for such a Biennial, as it was the sole institution in Washington capable of presenting such a large and ambitious art project. The Phillips Memorial Gallery (known today as the Phillips Collection) opened in 1922 as a pioneering museum of modern art, but its residential architecture and personal stylistic setting restricted the museum's ability to present large exhibitions of contemporary work and especially temporary, open-juried shows with hundreds of diverse objects. No other major museum of fine arts existed in the nation's capital until the National Gallery of Art opened in 1941. Even then, that federal museum generally avoided collecting and displaying contemporary art until its East Building was dedicated in 1978.[1] The Smithsonian Institution did not house the National Collection of Fine Arts (now the National Museum of American Art) in its own building until 1968; the Hirshhorn Museum and Sculpture Garden opened in 1974.

This local proliferation of museums is a major development of just the last thirty years. Washington now boasts a staggering array of cultural facilities, collections, and programming. This city today bears absolutely no resemblance to Washington at the dawn of this century. At that time, and for at least the next sixty years, the Corcoran's Biennial provided the only substantial arena in Washington to experience American contemporary painting.

At its inaugural exhibition in 1907, the Corcoran Biennial was visited by a remarkable two thousand people a day. The 1913 New York Armory Show created a heightened national awareness of progressive art in Europe and the United States. In its wake, press debates in Washington addressed the conservative and modernist forces shaping the Biennials. Public art sales of 297 paintings from the generally progressive 11th Biennial of 1928 totaled a stunning $500,000. This would amount to almost $5,000,000 in 1998 dollars.[2] Clearly, the public came to see the new art, the artists benefited from the Biennial, and acquisitions were made to private and public collections. From 1907 to 1940, when the Corcoran's grand spaces were entirely devoted to the Biennial, between three hundred and four hundred works were on view in these exhibitions. During the 1940s and 1950s, the Biennials ranged from two hundred to three hundred works. From the 1960s to 1995, one hundred or fewer paintings were shown each time. The evolution of professionalization, museum functions, and the roles of juries and curators that influenced the dynamics of these various Biennials are discussed elsewhere in this book.

A general survey of the pre-1969 years of the Biennial suggests a fluidity of process which guided the exhibiting, collecting, trading, and marketing of art. Before the jury programs ended in 1969, numerous artists repeatedly entered, or were invited to show, their latest works in Biennials. Participation became a badge of professional honor and an achievement that strengthened artists' bonds to the Corcoran. After 1969 this dynamic changed with the institution of curatorial selection.

THE COLLECTION

Regardless of these shifts in exhibition size, procedures, and themes, one enduring purpose of the Biennial has been to build the Corcoran's own permanent collection of paintings. It has served as the primary systematic and most persuasive mechanism by which the Corcoran has purchased contemporary paintings. In all, more than one-fifth of the works in our paintings collection has been acquired through Biennials. This is not a unique situation, since related ambitions to bring art into a city once underserved by commercial galleries also fueled Pittsburgh's triennial Carnegie International, founded in 1896. There, fully one-third of the Carnegie Museum of Art's collection of paintings and sculpture came from these juried exhibitions.[3] The Corcoran's Biennial encouraged the public to buy paintings as well, with the hope that these works might eventually be given back to the museum. Thus, the disciplined and consistent pattern of this museum-collecting process created a veritable time capsule of the artistic styles that have defined our common historical and cultural evolution in painting.

A survey of the Corcoran's acquisitions to its permanent collection provides an intriguing insight into twentieth-century art. From 1907 to 1995, the Corcoran acquired 223 works from various Biennials. The Gallery purchased at least one painting from every Biennial except four: those of 1979, 1983, 1985, and 1989. Directly or indirectly, the Corcoran acquired 177 of these works: 91 with moneys from the general Gallery Fund; 41 with museum endowment income from the William A. Clark Fund and 21 from the Anna E. Clark Fund; 14 with funds donated by the Friends of the Corcoran; and 9 with funds contributed by the Women's Committee. Largely before World War II, 20 works were subsequently exchanged with the original artists to upgrade their representation in the Corcoran's collection. Approximately two dozen other works were sold on the market, mostly in the 1940s, 1950s, and 1960s, to generate funds for art acquisitions. An additional 44 paintings ultimately came to the museum as gifts from private collectors or foundations. Nine more works were presented by artists, and 3 paintings were given by artists' families or friends.[4]

THE REALITIES

Every exhibition series of contemporary art seems condemned to suffer from instant analysis, appraisal against the past, counter-appraisal, and second-guessing. Biennial-type exhibitions seem to invite an "open season" of criticism. Such series offer that ritualistic time when both the official and the unofficial art world focuses on a targeted, discrete presentation of paintings. Public visitors weigh in by taking sides, finding favorites, or venting their own hostility. It is also a significant time for institutional posturing and arguing. Curiously, it may very well be that the ultimate purpose of Biennials is to stimulate just such contradictory but valuable dialogue and dynamic.

Biennials are obliged to operate without perspective. At best, they can be only an instant snapshot of curatorial or jury intuition, speculation, or taste. Only time will tell whether the brand-new art seen today will shape and push the history of art tomorrow. By that time, revision is impossible. It is far too late to patch the old wounds. If a goal of a Biennial is to establish some kind of order out of the relative chaos of new art, the exhibition is bound to leave some confusion, opinion, raw edges, and on occasion, professional discord. Such results are part of the evolving terrain of contemporary art.

THE FUTURE

From its founding in 1869 to the present, the Corcoran Gallery of Art has staged almost 1,800 special exhibitions. The vast majority of these have featured works by contemporary artists from the Washington region, the United States, or from numerous other nations. The Corcoran Biennials of "Oil Paintings by Contemporary American Artists" have long been a distinctive, recurring contemporary art event on the cultural calendar of both the museum and the city of Washington. During their early years, the Biennials were also the only time when the museum was substantially taken over for a large exhibition of new art. Following the general explosion and institutionalization of the avant-garde and contemporary American arts in the 1950s, however, the Biennials became just one of many such shows, not only at the Corcoran but elsewhere as well. Today, fully eighty percent of the Corcoran's special exhibition schedule is dedicated to the interpretation and display of contemporary art. Washington, and indeed the world, is saturated with all sorts of museums, galleries, alternative spaces, and exhibition agencies that generate an endless wave of exhibitions, catalogues, films, videos, and merchandise featuring contemporary art. The question thus arises, and remains ever-unanswerable: What can the Corcoran and its Biennials do to help the creation and appreciation of contemporary art?

In its earliest manifestations, the Corcoran Biennial was a fair reflection of the level, achievements, and interests of contemporary American painters. Yet we must concede that juried or institutionally curated exhibitions such as the Biennial are systemically unable to deal with the truly avant-garde. James Joyce's praise of "silence, exile, and cunning" expresses the self-imposed code of many avant-garde artists.[5] If we apply related words such as extremist, psychologically and socially militant, experimental, radical, bohemian, or independent, we further define the inherent problems. All extremist art is contemporary even if not all contemporary art is extremist. As these institutional exhibitions profess, Biennials and similar exhibitions are expected to present the "best" of new art (assuming that "best" can be identified). Some major works will nevertheless still fall outside immediate abilities to find them. We cannot assume that even the most brilliant generic exhibition can predictably find the cunning, silent, and exiled avant-garde painter, the best art, and potentially the most influential artists of the future.

Despite the odds and handicaps, the forty-four Biennials have served the Corcoran and Washington with dedication and enthusiasm over the years. A clear institutional commitment has remained, even as Biennials absorbed precious resources. With a millennial crossroads approaching, Jules Antoine Castagnary's historic thesis of the mid-nineteenth century still holds: art "is not at all an abstract conception, elevated above history . . .; it is part of the social consciousness, a fragment of the mirror in which the generations each look at themselves in turn, and as such it must follow society step by step, in order to take note of its incessant transformations."[6] It is essential that in the future, the new and increasingly flexible Corcoran Biennials be just such a mirror reflecting our evolving and equally fragmented contemporary cultures, regardless of the risk, confusion, and fractional nature of the product.[7]

ACKNOWLEDGMENTS

Senator William A. Clark, his wife Anna E. Clark, and their descendants deserve the most profound credit for perpetuating the Corcoran Biennial and its acquisition program throughout most of this century. In more recent times, all constituent groups and administrations of the Corcoran Gallery of Art have enthusiastically supported the Biennial and its acquisition program. We deeply appreciate the thoughtful and challenging discussions led by Corcoran Director and President David C. Levy. Since his arrival here in 1991, he has consistently tested exhibition committees by engaging the staff and Board of Trustees in the serious, if elusive and frustrating, question of how to distinguish the Biennial from any other large exhibition of contemporary art.

This current Biennial has benefited from the pioneering index work of curator Linda Crocker Simmons published in *The Biennial Exhibition Record of the Corcoran Gallery of Art 1907–1967*, which is unfortunately now out of print. Further, every office at the Corcoran has worked steadily over the last three years to shape and present this exhibition. While too numerous to list here, we acknowledge their essential support. Within the Museum Division, the exhibition's immediate curatorial team comprised Linda Crocker Simmons (Curator for American Art and Research), Terrie Sultan (Curator of Contemporary Art), and myself. We were assisted by, among others, Paige Turner and Laura Coyle (Assistant Curators of Exhibitions), Marisa Keller (Archivist), Lisa Ratkus (Design Director), Cristina Segovia (Rights and Reproductions Coordinator), Elizabeth Parr (Assistant to the Deputy Director and Chief Curator), Dare Harwell (Conservator), Susan Badder (Curator of Education), Cathy Crane Frankel (Exhibitions and Program Manager), Kirsten Verdi (Registrar), Victoria Fisher (Assistant Registrar), Clyde Paton (Senior Art Preparator), Greg Angelone (Assistant Preparator), and Ron Dees (docent volunteer).

Funding for this exhibition was provided by the Anna E. Clark endowment. The Kathrine Dulin Folger Fund and the Andrew W. Mellon Art Publications and Research Fund of the Corcoran Gallery of Art provided funds for this catalogue.

— J.C.

[1] See Philip Kopper, *America's National Gallery of Art: A Gift to the Nation* (New York: Harry N. Abrams, 1991), for much of the National Gallery's early history. Various exhibitions of works by wartime illustrators and painters were presented there in the 1940s, yet it was not until the 1963 bequest of the Chester Dale Collection that the National Gallery accommodated the permanent installation in its collections of works by living master artists (on the level of Picasso and Braque). Other artists were deferred until they had "passed the test of time." The need to commission living artists to decorate the new East Building in the mid-1970s definitively revised the National Gallery's program for both the acquisition and display of contemporary art.

[2] Todd Wilson at the Consumer Price Index of the Bureau of Labor Statistics supplied the figure of $4,742,690 for equivalent buying power today.

[3] John R. Lane et al., *Carnegie International* (Pittsburgh: Museum of Art, Carnegie Institute, 1985), pp. 10–15.

[4] Even with this current interpretive catalogue, an essential reference remains *The Biennial Exhibition Record of the Corcoran Gallery of Art 1907–1967*, ed. Peter Hasting Falk (Madison, Connecticut: Sound View Press, 1991). I thank and recognize Archivist Marisa Keller for her additional new research on the Corcoran's collection holdings acquired from all the Biennials from 1907 to 1995, which supports my analysis.

[5] Renato Poggioli, *The Theory of the Avant-Garde* (New York: Icon Editions, 1971), p. 3. See also James Joyce, *A Portrait of The Artist as a Young Man*, ed. Seamus Deane (London: Penguin Books, 1991), p. xxxiv.

[6] Jules Antoine Castagnary, "Salon de 1863," orginally published in *Le Nord* (Brussels: 1863), then reprinted in *Salons (1857–1870)* (Paris: Bibliothèque-Charpentier, 1892), I, pp. 102–106, translated and cited in Linda Nochlin, *Realism and Tradition in Art: 1848* (Englewood Cliffs, New Jersey: Prentice Hall, 1966), p. 64.

[7] In 1907 the Corcoran had neither curatorial departments nor curators responsible for prints, drawings, photography, or electronic media arts. The art then found in museums was dominantly painting on canvas, since the classical hierarchies of Art respected Painting as its most significant medium of expression. In response, the Corcoran School of Art developed a renown in teaching the disciplines and judgments inherent to the art of painting.

JOHN SINGER SARGENT
(1856–1925)

Mrs. Henry White, 1883

Oil on canvas

Gift of Mr. John
Campbell White

THE 6TH BIENNIAL

The Biennial Exhibitions: The First Sixty Years from 1907 to 1967

Linda Crocker Simmons, Curator for American Art and Research

On 1 January 1906, Frederick B. McGuire, the director of the Corcoran Gallery of Art, presented a proposal to the Gallery's Trustees for a competitive exhibition of contemporary American paintings.[1] The benefits he cited would be "three-fold: it would be of great advantage to the Gallery and a distinct factor in awakening public interest in it; it would prove highly beneficial to contributing artists; and at the same time, [it would] be instructive and interesting to art lovers, students, and the public at large."[2] He asserted that the Corcoran building could well accommodate such an exhibition by using the Atrium and the galleries around the second floor. McGuire also mapped out a dual process that allowed for the selection of artworks both by jury and by invitation. This stratagem was intended to ensure that some of the works shown would be by recognized painters who were well established in their careers but who might not wish to face the possible humiliation of being rejected by a jury. McGuire proposed writing to the most prominent artists in the country to solicit their works for the invitational section. These paintings would not be eligible to receive any awards or medals, while the uninvited works would be reviewed by panels of jurors who would choose those to be shown and awarded prizes. The jurors would be of further service by superintending the hanging of the exhibition. On a frugal note, McGuire suggested, "These juries will be invited to serve without compensation except of course the reimbursement of actual expenses."[3]

The Board of Trustees' acceptance of the proposed exhibition was a momentous one for the Corcoran. It was decided that the "First Exhibition of Contemporary American Paintings" would formally open with a "Private View and Reception" on the evening of 6 February 1907. The annual report gave a description of the evening: "The attendance included the President [Theodore] and Mrs. Roosevelt, members of the Cabinet, Senators and Representatives in Congress, Foreign Ambassadors, Ministers,

WINSLOW HOMER
(1836–1910)

A Light on the Sea, 1897
Oil on canvas
Museum Purchase,
Gallery Fund
THE 1ST BIENNIAL

Ralph Albert
Blakelock
(1847–1919)

Moonlight, c. 1890

Oil on canvas
William A. Clark
Collection

Part of Senator William
Clark Bequest to Corcoran
Gallery of Art in 1925

The 1st Biennial

many artists, art patrons, and connoisseurs, officers of the Army and Navy, and hundreds of others prominent in private and official life."[4] The opening of a Biennial exhibition soon evolved into a major event celebrated by Washington socialites and the regional art world alike.

The inaugural exhibition of 397 paintings attracted 62,697 persons over a period of 33 days. The exhibition filled all the galleries and the exterior space around the Atrium on the second floor of the building.[5] Twenty-six paintings on view were sold for a total of $49,000.[6] The thirteen paintings acquired for the Corcoran's permanent collection included examples of nineteenth-century academic traditions, such as James D. Smillie's *The Cliffs of Normandy,* and the heightened palette and broken brushstrokes associated with American impressionism, as seen in Childe Hassam's *Northeast Headlands – New England Coast.* Undoubtedly, the most significant purchase was Winslow Homer's magnificent *A Light on the Sea* which represents the artist's lifelong inquiry into the drama of man grappling with nature's power. His interpretation of this eternal conflict brought Homer to the attention of the next generation of American painters and laid a foundation for modernist movements. Such purchases underscored the Corcoran's commitment to the Biennial exhibitions, to its own American collection, and to contemporary American artists, a tradition that continues to this day.

In 1907, four separate juries of four men each, working in Boston, New York, Philadelphia, and Washington, made the initial selection of submitted works. Next, these sixteen jurors were narrowed to five—Irving R. Wiles,[7] Edmund C. Tarbell,[8] Hugh H. Breckinridge,[9] Frank Duveneck,[10] and Richard Norris Brooke[11]—who made the final decisions on awards and the hanging of paintings at the Corcoran.[12]

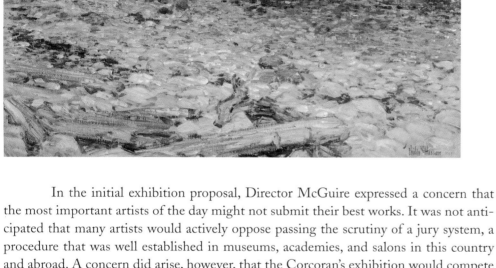

CHILDE HASSAM
(1859–1935)

*Northeast Headlands –
New England Coast*, 1901

Oil on canvas
Museum Purchase,
Gallery Fund
THE 1ST BIENNIAL

In the initial exhibition proposal, Director McGuire expressed a concern that the most important artists of the day might not submit their best works. It was not anticipated that many artists would actively oppose passing the scrutiny of a jury system, a procedure that was well established in museums, academies, and salons in this country and abroad. A concern did arise, however, that the Corcoran's exhibition would compete with other institutions for the best paintings. To counteract possible deficiencies, certain artists of recognized ability and reputation were invited to send recent work or requested paintings.

The two sections that comprised the Biennials for the next sixty years were thus established: one section of paintings submitted for selection by a jury and another section of invited works. Paintings in the second section, on view by special invitation, were not eligible to receive the prizes and medals awarded by the jury.[13] The first prize was to consist of $1,000 and a gold medal, the second prize of $500 and a silver medal, and the third prize of $250 and a bronze medal. Only oil paintings not previously exhibited in Washington were eligible for awards.

The multi-city system soon proved too cumbersome and was modified at the time of the 3rd Biennial (1910–11) in favor of a single jury. The invited section was retained, however, because it was considered an assurance of quality. It also provided a modest form of control through which the Corcoran could influence the content of the Biennials.

The first jurors and their successors were themselves practicing artists. Not until the 20th Biennial in 1947 did the director of the Corcoran (in this case Hermann Warner Williams) become a member of the jury.[14] Following this change the jury quick-

ly evolved into a group composed of Corcoran staff members—a curator, the director, and/or the principal of the School[15]—who were joined by museum professionals and art historians such as Lloyd Goodrich in 1949, Leslie Cheek in 1953, Theodore Rousseau, Jr. in 1957, and Charles E. Buckley in 1959. The makeup of these juries from 1907 until 1969 was almost exclusively white and male. The first and only woman to be included was Lillian Westcott Hale, who served in 1923 for the 9th Biennial.

The juries that selected paintings for the earliest Biennials left virtually no record of their decision-making processes. No comments by the jury were printed in the Biennial catalogues until 1949. Subsequent statements indicate that jurors felt their contemporaries were not submitting their best work. Director Williams noted that as an experiment, the 24th Biennial was open to all competitors. Of the 2,101 entries submitted, only 64 paintings were selected by the jury. Williams observed that "the staggeringly low percentage of successful entries suggests the unrewarding task that faced the jury." The jurors themselves expressed their concern. They were "troubled and perplexed that more painters of stature have not committed entries" and felt that the exhibition "could not be considered a balanced representation of American painting today."[16] Trends within the art world were leading away from the jury system and the awarding of prizes. These difficulties that faced Biennial juries from 1947 to 1967 led them to hedge their bets by offering honorable mention awards in addition to the three established Clark prizes.

Artist Edward Hopper stated in the jury's comment published in the catalogue for the 22nd Biennial in 1951: "As to the prize awards: The problems of prize awards is an old one, and most juries feel that the advancement of art is not furthered by the awarding of prizes. Even though one concedes there is a best picture or piece of sculpture in an exhibition, the fallibility of human judgment and the wide differences of opinion make the task of a just selection impossible, and the result must be unfair to many artists and misleading and confusing to the layman."[17]

Although the rules established for the first Biennial in 1907 applied to the exhibitions until 1969, over the years the balance between the number of juried works and the invited paintings changed. By the mid-1950s the bulk of the exhibition consisted of works by invited artists. In 1967, for the last exhibition to include a juried section, Director Williams observed in his catalogue essay:

> The 30th Biennial, as presented, represents only one of many possible solutions to the problem raised by a contemporary exhibition which is national in scope. This presentation is not comprehensive as, indeed, no exhibition of this type can be. It does, however, through the process of careful selection, show some 100 paintings which are the products of our time. The purpose of the exhibition is to present a group of works of high quality which show evidence of the creative mind at work. There is no conscious attempt to impose a strong point of view as to trends or tendencies. If such a point of view exists, it arises from the works themselves, not from the process by which they were selected.[18]

Beginning in 1969, the Biennial was transformed into an exhibition in which all works were submitted by invitation. The reasons for this change can be traced to

WILLARD LEROY
METCALF (1858–1925)

May Night, 1906

Oil on canvas
Museum Purchase,
Gallery Fund
First William A. Clark
Prize and Corcoran
Gold Medal
THE 1ST BIENNIAL

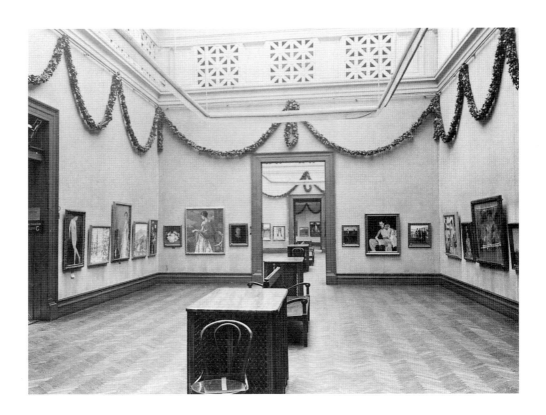

An installation view of the front galleries during the 11th Biennial, 1928

ARTHUR BOWEN DAVIES (1862–1928)

The Umbrian Mountains, 1925

Oil on canvas

Museum Purchase, William A. Clark Fund

THE 11TH BIENNIAL

developments in the art and museum fields during the mid-1960s. Further, it was believed that a jury's selection was unlikely to represent the highest level of current artistic activity. Finally, the costs and physical logistics of a nationwide, juried exhibition became increasingly impossible for one institution to undertake. In the Biennials held since 1967, the exhibitions were selected by the director, a member of the curatorial staff, or a guest curator. A more "conscious attempt [was made] to impose a strong point of view as to the trends and tendencies" of the times through the works selected. These recent Biennials have each borne the stamp of its organizer. Hopefully, each in its own way gives an overview of the concerns of the time. Only by selecting artists whose works represent the best and most interesting aspects of their time can the Corcoran continue to pursue the goal of its founder, William Wilson Corcoran, when he gave this institution the charge of "encouraging American genius, in the production and preservation of works pertaining to the Fine Arts and kindred objects."[19]

From the first Biennial exhibition to the 30th, the catalogues were modest in size and design.[20] Although the first catalogue was not illustrated, all successive ones contained a fair number of illustrations in black and white. Color was first featured in the catalogue of the 31st Biennial in 1969. Up until the early 1940s, the black-and-white illustrations in the catalogues were often grainy, fuzzy, and of generally poor quality. No surviving record indicates who was responsible for choosing the works to be illustrated. In the early catalogues, paintings that had been awarded prizes were so noted under the illustration. Beginning in 1919, with the catalogue of the 7th Biennial, prize winners were both illustrated and identified.[21] That catalogue was designed to guide visitors through the exhibition. Entries for the paintings were listed according to the arrangement in which the jury had installed them in the galleries. Each volume until the 21st Biennial of 1949 included an index of participating artists as well as a plan of the galleries. To help further educate gallery visitors, the Public Library of the District of Columbia published a pamphlet containing references to "Literature in Books and Periodicals on the Exhibitors" to accompany the Biennial exhibition.[22]

Individual labels with text identifying the artist and the painting's title were not used in the installations until sometime in the 1940s. Until that time the works had been identified by a number attached to the wall below the painting's frame. Visitors could purchase a copy of the catalogue to serve as a guide, or they could consult a catalogue hanging from a cord in the doorway of each room. The Corcoran had utilized this method since the late nineteenth century in an attempt to encourage catalogue sales.

Only a few photographs survive to show how the earliest Biennials were installed.[23] Available photographs indicate that the paintings were hung close together, with the bottom edges aligned at the same horizontal level. Garlands, apparently of cut greens, were draped above the paintings in continuous swags across the walls. Paintings appear to have been hung close to eye level for viewers of medium height. Very few works were double-hung in the salon style of the nineteenth century. Members of the jury, who supervised the installations, routinely determined positions of prominence along sight lines of the building, and articles in the press often noted the placement of favorite paintings.

Biennials from the 1940s through the 1960s were more innovative in their installations. Individual labels were placed beside each work, and paintings were more

ERNEST LAWSON
(1873–1939)

Boathouse, Winter,
Harlem River, 1916

Oil on canvas

Museum Purchase,
Gallery Fund

Second William A. Clark
Prize and Corcoran
Silver Medal

THE 6TH BIENNIAL

24

ELMER SCHOFIELD
(1867–1944)

Cliff Shadows, 1921

Oil on canvas

Museum Purchase,
Gallery Fund

THE 8TH BIENNIAL

widely spaced. Lowered track lighting was installed in most of the gallery spaces, and painted white walls replaced the dark fabrics that had been used earlier. In 1969, the spaces of the building itself played an important part in the success of the 31st Biennial. Director James Harithas was complimented for the strong interrelationship of architecture and large paintings throughout the second floor. Critics commented repeatedly on the light, color, and scale. "[Harithas] has offered the viewer not a lecture or a thesis, but an extraordinary visual voyage, an organized Odyssey whose separate adventure, merging in the memory, map the farthest reaches of non-representational painting of our day."[24] It was also for this Biennial that James Van Dijk painted a site-specific work on the walls of the Rotunda.[25]

In his initial proposal for the Biennial exhibition series, Director McGuire suggested that "prominent citizens" be asked to furnish funds for the three prizes that were to be offered. Accordingly, at the initial exhibition the funds for the first prize came from Senator William A. Clark,[26] the second prize from Charles C. Glover,[27] and the third prize from V. G. Fischer.[28] Even before the exhibition ended, Senator Clark offered the total prize money for the next Biennial, a practice he continued for a number of years. He later provided an endowment of $100,000 to perpetuate the William A. Clark Awards, which, with the accompanying medals, were given out at every Biennial through 1967. In 1927 Anna E. Clark, the senator's widow, established a similar endowment of $100,000, with its income designated to meet the expenses of organizing the Biennial exhibitions. The surplus income from both funds has been used to purchase works by

26

MARY STEVENSON
CASSATT (1844–1926)

*Susan on a Balcony
Holding a Dog*, c. 1880

Oil on canvas
Museum Purchase,
Gallery Fund

THE 2ND BIENNIAL

American artists for the Corcoran's permanent collection.

One of the original goals of the Biennial was to better familiarize the public with American art and its current directions. To generate public interest and encourage a more careful look at the paintings, Corcoran director C. Powell Minnigerode established the Popular Prize during the 6th Biennial of 1916. As the name implies, this award of $200 went to the artist whose painting received the most votes cast by visitors attending the exhibition. The selection became a popular pastime for visitors and attracted considerable press comment regarding the recipient's merit, or apparent lack thereof. Interestingly, no Popular Prize ever went to any of the prize winners selected by the jury or to any work that could be remotely identified as modern. In the thirteen Biennials during which the Popular Prize was awarded—it ended with the start of World War II—three artists were frequent winners: William M. Paxton, Gari Melchers, and N. C. Wyeth.

Collectors from the Washington region and beyond were encouraged to purchase paintings from the Biennials. From the time of the first Biennial in 1907, each catalogue indicated which works were for sale, and purchases were often brisk. Some of the paintings eventually came back to the Gallery—whether as a gift, exchange, or bequest. George M. Oyster, Jr., a wealthy Washington businessman, dairy owner, and philanthropist, acquired many paintings directly from Biennials. After his death in April 1921, the first codicil to his will gave the Corcoran its choice of the American paintings in his collection. From that selected group of six works, four had been in Biennials: *Overlooking the Valley* by Edward Redfield (8th Biennial of 1921), *Josephine Knitting* by Edmund C. Tarbell (6th Biennial of 1916), and *Obeweebetuck* by Julius Alden Weir and *Old House at Easthampton* by Childe Hassam (both in the 7th Biennial of 1919). Duncan Phillips, a noted Washington collector, (whose own museum, now called The Phillips Collection, opened in 1922) made a number of purchases from Biennials. He kept some works, but he presented two paintings to the Corcoran: *The Smithy* by Gari Melchers from the 3rd Biennial in 1910, and *Fruit Bowl* by Harold Weston from the 19th Biennial in 1945 (both given in 1950).

Corcoran trustees acquired paintings from the Biennials and also lent works to the exhibitions. James Parmelee, a Corcoran trustee from 1916 to 1931, bequeathed to the Gallery one such group of paintings by American artists. The bequest included *Simplon Pass* by John Singer Sargent, which Parmelee had lent to the 5th Biennial of 1914–15, and *The Picture from Thibet* by Emil Carlsen which appeared in the 10th Biennial of 1926.

On occasion, artists also made gifts of works shown in the Biennials. Louis Betts and George Biddle, for example, gave portraits. Betts presented *Yvonne*, a portrait of the daughter of fellow painter, Guy Pénè du Bois, which had appeared in the 9th Biennial of 1923. Biddle gave a portrait of his wife Helene Sardeau, a noted sculptor, which had been shown in the 15th Biennial of 1937.

From their beginning, the Biennial exhibitions were intended to present the myriad facets and finest examples of contemporary American painting. This challenge made the exhibitions and their catalogues a chronicle of the various developments of American art from 1907 to the present day. A survey of the exhibitions offers some insight into contemporary artistic taste. In examining an index of the artists who exhib-

ited during this sixty-year period, it is surprising to note that many of the names are largely unfamiliar today. Some of these artists and their works will need the benefit of time before their talents are once again recognized. Apart from these unknowns, however, a considerable number of these painters are still highly regarded, and their presence in the Biennials is naturally expected.

From an initial examination of the catalogues it appears that the Biennial juries selected works by some of the finest living artists of their day. The list of names reads like a section from *Who Was Who in American Art*: Thomas Eakins, Albert Pinkham Ryder, Ralph Albert Blakelock, John Singer Sargent, Childe Hassam, George Bellows, George Luks, Edward Hopper, Edmund C. Tarbell, Raphael Soyer, Robert Henri, Maurice Prendergast, John Sloan, Marsden Hartley, John Marin, Yasou Kuniyoshi, and many others. With the distance of several decades, however, it is apparent that the Biennial choices were, for their time, often conservative and generally late to acknowledge the existence of certain contemporary art movements. Little awareness of European movements such as post-impressionism, cubism, and futurism was evident in the works displayed. The conservative nature of the selections is even more apparent in the treatment of such developments as American impressionism, the "Ash Can" school, regionalism or the American scene, abstract expressionism, pop and op art—even the Washington Color School—which often were recognized years after they first emerged.

A preponderance of still life and landscape subjects was common from 1907 through the 1930s. This well may have reflected a Washington preference and the collecting habits of William Wilson Corcoran as evident in his founding gift.

The earliest Biennials were rich in landscapes. Notable purchases from them

included works by Daniel Garber, George Symons, Emil Carlsen, Ernest Lawson, and John Singer Sargent.

From the very first Biennial the Corcoran either purchased or received as a gift or a bequest at least one work from every Biennial exhibition until the 36th Biennial in 1979. Childe Hassam's *Northeast Headlands – New England Coast* of 1901 and Mary Cassatt's *Susan on a Balcony with a Dog* of circa 1880 were purchased from the first and second Biennials respectively. Both artists had integrated the broken brushstrokes and heightened palette of French impressionism into their work to produce a distinctive style.

Of the two painters, Cassatt was truer to her French associates and their ideas. A friend of artist Edgar Degas, she exhibited her work with him and other impressionists throughout the late nineteenth century. Flashes of blues, pinks, and silvery purple combine with white in the glowing gown worn by the model, who holds a little griffin dog on her lap. Behind her, the rooftops of Paris blur atmospherically as touches of the same pigments combine with flashes of red and green. Cassatt's artistic abilities were equal if not superior, to most of the French impressionists with whom she exhibited. Her paintings appeared in Biennials until 1926, but she never received an award.

Hassam employed fragmented strokes of paint like those he had observed during visits to studios and galleries in France during the 1880s and later. By the late nineteenth century, his style demonstrated a knowledge of the dappling light effects created by shortened brush strokes. This technique caused the rocky permanence of the headland almost to dissolve into shimmering colors. This work retains a sense of physical permanence, however, and throughout his career that aspect set him apart from his French inspiration. At heart, Hassam seems to have loved the solidity of his subjects, whether

CHILDE HASSAM
(1859–1935)

*Old House at
Easthampton,* 1916

Oil on canvas
Bequest of George
M. Oyster, Jr.

THE 7TH BIENNIAL

they were coastal scenes or old New England houses, such as *Old House at Easthampton,* which was exhibited in the 7th Biennial in 1919 and acquired by the Corcoran through a bequest in 1924. Hassam continued to exhibit in the Biennials until his death in 1935. In that time he received two awards: a third prize in the 3rd Biennial in 1910 and a first prize in the 4th Biennial of 1912 for *The New York Window,* which the Corcoran purchased.

Daniel Garber's *April Landscape,* a lovely, atmospheric view of a Pennsylvania quarry near New Hope, was purchased from the 3rd Biennial of 1910, the second time the ever-popular artist participated in the Biennials. A total of thirty-eight of his paintings were shown in twenty exhibitions, during which time he received three prizes and accompanying medals. Garber also served as a juror three times. In 1921, eleven years later, the Corcoran purchased his *South Room – Green Street* from the 8th Biennial. Such lyrical interpretations of the landscape are intensified in Emil Carlsen's *Moonlight on a Calm Sea,* purchased from the 6th Biennial of 1916. The misty colors rising from a tran-

quil sea reveal an exotic strain in Carlsen's style traced to his interest in Asian aesthetics and objects. Even the vertical format may have been selected in response to the hanging scrolls that are so prevalent in Japanese and Chinese painting.

A very impressionist approach to landscape subjects, albeit a river scene, is seen in Ernest Lawson's *Boathouse, Winter, Harlem River,* which was shown in the 6th Biennial in 1916 and won the second prize and medal. The thick, active paint application so distinctive of Lawson's style creates the visual effect of crushed, glimmering jewels.

Brilliance of light and clarity of color also distinguish the work of landscape painter George Gardner Symons, who exhibited thirteen paintings in various Biennials. The Corcoran purchased *Where Long Shadows Lie* from the 7th Biennial of 1919. Vibrant with glowing sunshine, the painting's colors capture the effect of reflected light and luminosity often seen on a clear day after a snowfall. This work stands out as one of the finest of the surprisingly high number of snow scenes acquired from the Biennials.[29]

Beyond a doubt, one of the most dynamic landscapes exhibited in the 5th

Biennial in 1914 was *Simplon Pass* by John Singer Sargent. The artist employed vigorous brushwork to capture this sun-drenched scene with water splashing over boulders. He preserved for all time a region of southern Switzerland where he enjoyed vacationing with family and friends. Sargent, then at the height of his mature creative powers, was repeatedly invited to submit such paintings in order to maintain a high level of quality in the Biennials.

American impressionists had struggled for acceptance in the latter decades of the nineteenth century, yet Biennial juries only grudgingly granted approval to them in the early Biennials. In the following decades, Childe Hassam, Willard Metcalf, and Julian Weir participated in all the Biennials, and they continued to receive Biennial prizes for as long as they painted.

As the result of the Corcoran's Biennial purchases, American impressionists are well represented in the collection. Frederick C. Frieseke, an expatriate American active in France for four decades, enjoyed a popular following in the Biennials, exhibiting thirty-one works in the 2nd through the 16th Biennial, including three prize-winning entries. *Peace,* purchased from the 8th Biennial in 1921, shows Sarah Ann, the artist's wife and frequent model, sewing in the corner of a room by a baby bassinet. Frieseke's delicate froth of pastels applied in semi-pointillist daubs of pigment combine with charming touches, such as the bouquet of flowers and the decoration on the bassinet, to create a tranquil environment of feminine intimacy—a stylistic hallmark.

Maurice Prendergast exhibited eight paintings in as many Biennials, receiving the third prize and a medal for *Landscape with Figures* from the 9th Biennial of 1923. Prendergast painted this work in his intensely personal style, employing a mosaic of fragmented colors to form

WILLIAM GLACKENS
(1870–1938)

Luxembourg Gardens,
1906

Oil on canvas
Museum Purchase,
William A. Clark Fund

THE 15TH BIENNIAL

34

JOHN SLOAN
(1871–1951)

Yeats at Petitpas, 1910

Oil on canvas
Museum Purchase,
Gallery Fund

THE 13TH BIENNIAL

bands of figures, trees, and water. On his first trip to Paris in 1891, he encountered the modernist currents of the post-impressionists, Nabis and Symbolists, and began to depict the human form as color shapes enlivening urban settings such as parks and boulevards or on holiday outings in the country. The distance and isolation of the featureless figures moves the work beyond nineteenth-century considerations of impressionism into modernist concerns with color patterns and abstract forms.

Like Prendergast, Arthur Bowen Davies was well represented by seventeen paintings in eleven Biennials, including *Umbrian Mountains* and *Stars and Dews and Dreams of Night,* both of which were shown in the 11th Biennial of 1928. Typical of the subject matter that dominated the artist's later years, these two works were created in the highly decorative style that Davies followed throughout much of his career, except for a brief deviation into cubism in the years following the 1913 International Exhibition of Modern Art, popularly known as the Armory Show. In his mature paintings dreamlike figures rendered in pearly flesh tones are arranged in a frieze of quietly dancing forms. In his late landscapes, such as *Umbrian Mountains*, thinly painted calligraphic brushstrokes define the geological features of the land. This is Davies at his finest.

Portraiture was a perennial favorite of the juries and the public alike. John Singer Sargent, liked by the press and public, was invited to send paintings to many of the early Biennials. The 6th Biennial of 1916 included eighteen canvases by him, while the 7th Biennial of 1919 featured his portrait of John D. Rockefeller in a place of prominence. Sargent and Melchers were possibly the two most popular and critically acclaimed artists throughout the first decade of the Biennials. Other beloved painters included Daniel Garber, Ernest Lawson, and Childe Hassam, whose portraits and landscapes painted

LEFT:
GARI MELCHERS
(1860–1932)

The Smithy, 1910

Oil on canvas
Gift of Duncan Phillips
THE 3RD BIENNIAL

RIGHT:
ROBERT HENRI
(1865–1929)

Indian Girl in White Ceremonial Blanket,
c. 1921

Oil on canvas
Museum Purchase, Gallery Fund
THE 9TH BIENNIAL

en plein air regularly won prizes at various exhibitions held throughout the United States. Their subjects and styles of painting were recognizable, appealing, and attractive to collectors. Hassam alone is said to have won thirty-three medals and prizes in his lifetime, including the William A. Clark Prize and Gold Medal at the 4th Biennial for the painting *The New York Window,* which was purchased from that exhibition for the Corcoran's permanent collection.

Works by Sloan, Henri, Luks, and their associates of The Eight and the Ash Can school also began to be shown during the 1910s and were continually featured throughout their lives. In 1932, Luks, at the age of sixty-five years, was the only one of this group to receive the First Clark Prize and award for his *Woman with Black Cat.*

Women were not well represented in the early Biennials, and only a few paintings by women were purchased during the first sixty years. Mary Cassatt was an obvious choice, as was Cecilia Beaux, who is considered one of America's finest women portraitists at the turn of the century. Isabel Bishop, active much later in the century, is a third. In Beaux's portrait *Sita and Sarita,* a replica of an earlier painting sold to the French Government in 1921, the sitters are Sarah A. Leavitt (Mrs. Walter Turle) and her pet cat. (It has never been entirely certain which one is nicknamed Sita and which one is Sarita.) Both sitters are delineated in Beaux's rich, fluid brushwork as seen in the shades of the white dress set off against a patterned fabric chair. In addition to being technically masterful in the use of paint, Beaux was a keen observer of character, both human and feline, giving each sitter her own personality.

Works included in the 6th Biennial, held on the eve of World War I, offered only the broadest hints of modernism to that time. Paintings by Max Weber, Arthur B. Carles, Arthur Bowen Davies, and Maurice Prendergast were progressive choices. Weber's *Still Life*, although not illustrated in the Biennial catalogue and unlocated today, is likely to have shown the influence of cubism, which had shaped his style in preceding years.[30] Avant-garde artists who responded to European developments did not always fare well either. Arthur Dove, a radical painter, never exhibited a work in the Biennial. John Marin did not participate in a Biennial until 1949, twelve years after his 1937 retrospective was held at the Museum of Modern Art in New York. Other aesthetic biases on the part of jury members from the late 1920s through the 1930s can be deduced by the scarcity of works by artists such as Joseph Stella, Stanton McDonald-Wright, and Georgia O'Keeffe.[31]

In their own organizations, Washington artists demonstrated a predilection for the same subject matter. The faculty of the Corcoran School of Art was often successful with their submissions to the Biennials. Works by Eugen Weisz, Richard Lahey, Catherine Critcher, Mitchell Jamieson, Edmund C. Tarbell, and Richard Meryman were frequently included. The first faculty member to win a Biennial prize and medal was Samuel Burtis Baker, for his painting *Interior with Figure* in the 8th Biennial of 1921.

Baker is one of the few Corcoran faculty members from the early decades of the Biennials to have had a painting purchased by the Gallery. *Interior with Figure* was acquired in 1936, fifteen years after the work was shown in the 8th Biennial. Trained in

Boston, Baker had followed Tarbell to Washington to teach at the Corcoran School of Art. He continued to live in the area even after his Corcoran teaching career ended.

Corcoran students were not selected as often, but among those whose paintings were accepted by the jury were: Olive Rush, Gladys Nelson Smith, Mae Jurow, and Eben Commins.[32] Artists of the Washington area fared a little better than Corcoran students. Noted among those who exhibited in various Biennials are Richard Norris Brooke, Edgar Nye, Sarah M. Baker, William H. Calfee, Charles Bittinger, Bjorn P. Egeli, and Robert Franklin Gates.

The 11th Biennial of 1928 and the 12th Biennial of 1930 saw modernism gain a slightly stronger hold. Barnard Karfiol's painting, *Summer*, received the First Prize in the 11th Biennial, while Maurice Sterne's painting, *After Lunch*, took the same prize in the 12th. Increasingly, paintings with modernist stylistic developments and interpretations of subjects were more likely to receive prizes.

Political issues only occasionally affected the Biennials. In 1939, Stuart Davis, Rockwell Kent, Max Weber, and other artists were joined by a number of arts organizations in protesting the exclusion of an anti-Fascist painting by Peter Blume from the exhibition. Even though the painting—a caricature of Italian Fascist leader Benito Mussolini overlooking Rome—had been rejected by the Biennial jury in open competition, the Corcoran administration was accused of harboring Fascist sympathies. The Corcoran issued a statement that the jury had rejected the painting on its artistic merits alone. C. Powell Minnigerode, the Corcoran's director, had been worried about the possibility of the painting being accepted by the jury, and he had asked the State Department to issue a letter restricting its exhibition. Ultimately, the State Department, fearing criticism, refused to become involved. The work was not shown, but paintings by Blume were included in the 20th Biennial in 1947 and the 25th Biennial in 1957.

Rockwell Kent's political views limited his opportunities to exhibit regularly after World War II. His membership in the Socialist party, as well as his outspoken opposition to modern art, led to his disfavor in art circles. Before 1939, however, he showed ten works in as many Biennials, and his painting *Adirondacks,* was purchased from the 13th Biennial of 1932. Kent was a popular illustrator and printmaker known for his stark images of Greenland, Newfoundland, and Tierra del Fuego. This scene in New York, not far from the artist's dairy farm in AuSable, captures many of the qualities he seemed to love in the open, windblown regions he often depicted.

The Great Depression affected Philip Evergood profoundly. Through the guise of everyday scenes, he examined issues of race discrimination, political oppression, and a wide array of social ills that plagued Americans. His style varied, but it often retained an expressionistic use of black lines and brilliant hues. *Sunny Side of the Street* purchased from the 22nd Biennial in 1951, celebrates the great diversity of American society as encapsulated in a crowded street scene in Brooklyn, where the artist once lived.

Wartime conditions in 1943 excluded the possibility of having more than two thousand paintings shipped to Washington for jury consideration. Instead, the final exhibition, which included 264 paintings (primarily of invited works) was brought to the Gallery by van. Artists within a twenty-mile radius of the Corcoran were permitted to submit works to the jury. Preoccupation with the war effort lessened press coverage of the show. The 19th Biennial in 1945 faced similar shipping difficulties and consisted

JOHN SINGER SARGENT
(1856–1925)

Simplon Pass, 1911

Oil on canvas

Bequest of James Parmelee

THE 5TH BIENNIAL

FREDERICK FRIESEKE
(1874–1939)

Peace, 1917

Oil on canvas

Museum Purchase,
Gallery Fund

THE 8TH BIENNIAL

40

MAURICE
PRENDERGAST
(1859–1924)

Landscape with Figures,
1921

Oil on canvas

Museum Purchase,
William A. Clark Fund

Third William A. Clark
Prize and Corcoran
Bronze Medal

THE 9TH BIENNIAL

ARTHUR BOWEN DAVIES
(1862–1928)

*Stars and Dews and
Dreams of Night*, 1927

Oil on canvas
Museum Purchase,
William A. Clark Fund

THE 11TH BIENNIAL

42

mostly of invited works.

Biennials in the late 1940s saw the inclusion of paintings by many more artists working in abstract styles. Sigmund Menkes's *Days End,* shown in the 20th Biennial in 1947, was the first work in an abstract style to win first prize and a gold medal. In the 1950s, even more artists working in abstract styles, most notably abstract expressionism, were selected. A critic for the *New York Times* observed in 1952 that the general field of straight realism continued to dominate most of the Biennials "with occasional examples of expressionism or abstraction appearing a little lost in the general effect."[34]

By mid-century, some artists noted with regret and opposition the inroads being made by modernism to the exclusion of their own work from the Biennials. Press commentary further conceded that the layman found the innovative stylistic concepts of certain artists too modern or confusing to appreciate or understand. It clearly had become difficult to satisfy all participants—jurors, artists, and viewers alike—as the Biennial approached its fiftieth year.

In their statement for the 22nd Biennial in 1951, jurors Edward Hopper, John C. Johansen, and Eugen Weisz criticized the practice of awarding prizes and suggested that a system of purchase awards would eliminate "the grading according to merit of the prize system and the implication of superiority."

The catalogue preface for the 24th Biennial of 1955 described how the institution attempted to deal with continued negative comments about the two-part system. That Biennial "differed from the previous ones in that it was an open competition with no invited participants . . . [an action taken] in an effort to accede to the desire of a majority of artists who believe that an open competition gives a better chance to

SAMUEL BURTIS BAKER
(1882–1967)

Interior with Figure, 1920

Oil on canvas
Museum Purchase,
William A. Clark Fund
Second William A. Clark
Prize and Corcoran
Silver Medal

THE 8TH BIENNIAL

43

EDMUND CHARLES
TARBELL (1862–1938)

Josephine Knitting, 1916

Oil on canvas
Bequest of George M.
Oyster, Jr.
THE 6TH BIENNIAL

the younger and lesser-known among them."[35] The jury reviewed 2,101 paintings but accepted only 64. A breakdown of the geographical distribution of accepted entries revealed that the largest group came from metropolitan New York, followed by Washington, DC. The rest of the entries were sent from nearly every state. Unfortunately, regional diversity did not guarantee that the best-known artists entered or that the highest quality of paintings were submitted. The jurors observed: "[We] were troubled and perplexed that more painters of stature have not contributed entries. This leads us to question whether an open competition is the most satisfactory method of securing a nationally representative exhibition of the highest caliber. In effect we believe that the 24th Biennial is one of high quality, but that it cannot be considered a balanced representation of American painting today."[36] Thus the first peals of a death knell sounded over the Biennial jury and prize systems.

Despite these dire warnings, the names of artists included in the 24th Biennial offer an interesting perspective on contemporary art at mid-century. Many remain as unknown today as they were to the jurors more than forty years ago, yet adventuresome works such as Willem de Kooning's *Woman VI*, Franz Kline's *Painting 1953*, and Richard Diebenkorn's *Berkeley-No. 6* were featured. The Corcoran purchased the third prize winner, Larry Rivers's *Self-Figure* (1955). This acquisition signaled the Gallery's intent to pursue the avant-garde. In *Self-Figure*, Rivers bridges the terrain between the painterly gestures of abstract expressionism and the straightforwardness of pop iconography. With its loosely rendered gestures and media-based approach to representation,

BERNARD KARFIOL
(1886–1952)

Summer, 1927

Oil on canvas
Museum Purchase,
William A. Clark Fund
First William A. Clark
Prize and Corcoran
Gold Medal
THE 11TH BIENNIAL

Self-Figure brought a thoroughly modern approach to figurative representation to the Gallery's collection.

Composed of two distinct parts—a historical section and a contemporary section—the 25th Biennial of 1957 provided an opportunity to survey the impact and influence of the past Biennials. The historical section had two components: one made exclusively of the canvases that had received the first prize, and the other devoted to works that had been exhibited but not awarded prizes. In his essay "Fifty Years of Biennial Exhibitions," director Hermann Warner Williams observed that, "the Biennial series is no longer needed to demonstrate the validity of American painting, but it still can serve its original secondary function: to encourage its development."[37] Williams also acknowledged that "the percentage of 'successes' to 'failures' appears to be remarkably consistent throughout the early period of the series. It may be assumed that it persists to the present."[38]

The contemporary section of 239 paintings included a number of works by artists associated with abstract expressionism, which was then being recognized as a major American style. Among the artists invited to participate were Ad Reinhardt, Josef Albers, William Baziotes, Richard Diebenkorn, Hans Hofmann, and Andrew Wyeth. From this varied group the Corcoran elected to buy two pieces, one of which was Josef Albers's *Homage to the Square: "Yes"* of 1956. Winner of the Third Clark Prize and Corcoran Bronze Medal, it is a prime example of Albers's late paintings, collectively entitled *Homage to the Square.* With this series, Albers embarked on an extended, highly refined exploration of color theory and abstract geometry for which he is well known.

The 26th Biennial in 1959 saw a return to the juried system and invited sections, with 134 paintings in the invited section and a smaller juried section of 53 works. Again, the complaint was made that poor quality works had been submitted but it was reiterated that "the Gallery has an obligation to continue having a juried section despite the small return, or the time, effort and expense entailed."[39]

Joining the Gallery's growing collection of pure geometric abstraction was Will Barnet's *Multiple Images I* (1959), a jazzy, syncopated composition that explores abstract forms extrapolated from actual experience. Rooted in cubism and closely related to paintings by Stuart Davis, the figure/ground relationship between the images and the spatial environment is flattened and rational. Barnet's high-keyed color further enhances the form, creating a retinal interplay that is an integral part of the overall composition. *Multiple Images I* received the Third Clark Prize and Corcoran Bronze Medal in 1961.

Lee Bontecou's *Untitled (57)* of 1961 challenges the accepted boundary between painting and sculpture. Constructed of welded metal and painted canvas, it breaks down the tradition of a flat, painted picture plane. Spatially complex and richly textured, this monochromatic work hovers between natural and mechanized environments. By establishing a circular void as the compositional focal point, Bontecou draws the viewer's eye into a complex interplay between foreground and background. A precursor to both Robert Mangold and Elizabeth Murray (who exhibited in the 40th Biennial), Bontecou was awarded second prize for *Untitled (57)*, a validation of her innovative approach to painting.

PHILIP EVERGOOD
(1901–1973)

Sunny Side of the Street,
1950

Egg-oil-varnish emulsion
with marble dust and glass
on canvas

Museum Purchase,
Anna E. Clark Fund

Second William A. Clark
Prize and Corcoran
Silver Medal

THE 22ND BIENNIAL

LARRY RIVERS
(B. 1923)

Self-Figure, 1955

Oil on canvas

Museum Purchase,
William A. Clark Fund

Third William A. Clark
Prize and Corcoran
Bronze Medal

THE 24TH BIENNIAL

WILL BARNET
(B. 1911)

Multiple Images I, 1959

Oil on canvas

Museum Purchase,
Anna E. Clark Fund

Third William A. Clark
Prize and Corcoran
Bronze Medal

THE 27TH BIENNIAL

First Theme, a fine example of Burgoyne Diller's colorful, hard-edged abstraction, finds its roots in the late work of Dutch artist Piet Mondrian. The purity of form and color—four unequal zones of red, blue, yellow, and white appear on a flat, black field—results in a dynamic compositional exploration of balance. This early expression of a minimalist approach to painting dovetails well with Josef Albers's *Homage to the Square: "Yes,"* acquired from the 25th Biennial.

The first four Biennials of the 1960s—the 27th in 1961, the 28th in 1963, the 29th in 1965, and the 30th in 1967—continued to struggle with issues that had plagued similar juried exhibitions over the past decade. The unwillingness of some artists to participate in such exhibitions was noted. Director Williams explained the absence of painters Clyfford Still and Mark Rothko from the Biennials as being their choice not to participate in group exhibitions.[40] For the 27th Biennial, the Corcoran changed the initial selection process. Rising financial costs and the physical logistics of transporting thousands of entries were fast becoming limiting factors in continuing a national survey show.

The solution—to accept the submission of slides for the initial jury selection—was met with widespread comment and opposition. From the three thousand slides received, 125 paintings were brought to the Gallery for viewing by the jurors. Thirty-five paintings were chosen from this group. This selection method continued to be used throughout the 1960s. A number of changes in style were observed during this decade. Abstract Expressionism, which had achieved almost a national status, began to be less prominent except on the regional level. Pop and op art remained popular along with hard-edge abstraction. Local developments of the Washington Color School

BURGOYNE DILLER
(1906–1965)

First Theme, c. 1962

Oil on canvas
Gift of the Ford
Foundation
THE 28TH BIENNIAL

received modest attention. Morris Louis showed a painting only once, in the 29th Biennial of 1965, while Kenneth Noland fared better with works included in three Biennials. Gene Davis and Thomas Downing each participated twice. Lacking formal art training, Davis did not start painting until the 1950s after a career as a journalist. For much of the 1960s and the 1970s he produced signature paintings of hard-edge vertical stripes which were intended to allow the canvas to serve as a vehicle just for the appreciation of color. Although a fair number of the painters associated with the Washington Color School such as Gene Davis, Kenneth Noland, Thomas Downing, Morris Louis, and Paul Reed participated in the Biennials, very few of their works were purchased from the exhibitions. Instead, they were acquired for the collection later and in other ways.

Following the 30th Biennial of 1967, some of the changes that had been fore-shadowed in the previous two decades were finally permanently instituted. The jury system was abolished, and along with it, the practice of conferring prize awards and medals. Biennials of the next thirty years were governed by different principles and practices. Even so, the Biennials continued to grow and exert their critical importance in the art world. As Hermann Warner Williams, Jr. remarked in his essay for the 25th Biennial, the purpose of the exhibitions was to prove to the country "the just claim of American Art to rank with the best in the world . . . and to encourage its further development . . . ."[41] Critical comments from the press, museum professionals, and artists substantiated the success of the Biennial. The depth and magnitude of the Corcoran's collection of American paintings from the first half of the twentieth century further confirm the Biennial's importance and the achievement of its goals.

The Biennials also benefited the institution in the growth and development of its permanent collection, which during the first half of the century was directly allied to these exhibitions. When conservative views reigned, similarly oriented works were acquired by the Corcoran. When dynamic changes occurred in the art world, they were reflected both in the exhibitions and in the art acquired.

By the end of the 1960s, the Biennial had achieved many of its original goals. In supporting American painting, it reflected the logical developments and surprising vagaries of the contemporary art world. Despite many challenges, the Biennial responded to changes in the art world by adapting and reinventing itself as a vital part of the Corcoran's ongoing commitment to contemporary American painting.

— L.C.S.

JOSEF ALBERS
(1888–1976)

Homage to the Square: "Yes", 1956

Casein on masonite

Museum Purchase,
William A. Clark Fund

Third William A. Clark
Prize and Corcoran
Bronze Medal

THE 25TH BIENNIAL

LEE BONTECOU
(B. 1931)

Untitled (57), 1961

Welded metal and
painted canvas

Gift of the Ford
Foundation

Second William A.
Clark Prize and the
Corcoran Silver Medal

THE 28TH BIENNIAL

[1] This essay first appeared in *The Biennial Exhibition Record of the Corcoran Gallery of Art 1907–1967,* ed. Peter Hasting Falk (Madison, Connecticut: Sound View Press, 1991). It has been revised and is published here with the permission of Peter Hasting Falk of Sound View Press. Significant additions were written and researched by Marisa Keller, Corcoran Archivist.

[2] Proposal presented by F. B. McGuire to the Board of Trustees, 1 January 1906, Corcoran Gallery of Art, Archives of the Corcoran Gallery and School of Art (hereafter CGSA Archives).

[3] Ibid.

[4] *Annual Report of the Director of the Corcoran Gallery of Art* (Washington, DC: Corcoran Gallery of Art, 1908), p. 14.

[5] The present Corcoran building was designed by Ernest Flagg. The cornerstone was laid in 1893 and construction was completed in 1897. The Clark wing and the Gallery addition designed by Charles Platt were begun in 1925 and completed in 1927.

[6] "The Record of Pictures Sold" (manuscript ledger, CGSA Archives) begins with the first exhibition and continues through the 19th Biennial in 1945. The title, artist, entry number, purchaser, and price paid for each work are recorded.

[7] Irving R. Wiles (1861–1948), son of landscape painter Lemuel Maynard Wiles, was an illustrator, portrait painter, and member of many artists' organizations.

[8] A member of the artists' group known as "The Ten," Edmund C. Tarbell (1862–1938) had taught at the School of the Museum of Fine Arts, Boston since 1888. He served as principal of the Corcoran School of Art from 1918 until 1926.

[9] Hugh H. Breckinridge (1870–1937) was an instructor at the Pennsylvania Academy of Fine Arts as well as a widely exhibited painter in oil and watercolor.

[10] Frank Duveneck (1848–1919), a Cincinnati artist, was a widely exhibited painter, sculptor, and printmaker.

SUE FULLER (B. 1914)

String Composition #144, 1967

Nylon threads under Plexiglass

Gift of Mr. Emerson Crocker

THE 29TH BIENNIAL

[11] A painter and teacher, Richard Norris Brooke (1847–1920) was Vice Principal of the Corcoran School of Art (1902–18). He was closely identified with art interests and organizations in the nation's capital.

[12] Many Biennial jurors, including these five for the first Biennial, are represented by works in the Corcoran's collection. They also participated as exhibitors in other Biennial presentations.

[13] Works not eligible to receive awards were identified by a symbol in the catalogue. Exceptions to this two-part system were occasionally made; the 20th (1947) and 21st (1949) Biennials had no jury sections, only invited works. This temporary change was necessitated by restricted shipping conditions during World War II. The 24th Biennial of 1955 was the only one before 1969 to include only a juried section.

[14] The juries for the first five Biennials worked under the direction of a supervising committee made up of Corcoran staff and a trustee. Although the name of no Corcoran staff or trustee is listed in the catalogues after that date, it is clear from the records that C. Powell Minnigerode, director from 1916 to 1947, was actively involved in the selection process and exerted a strong influence. On occasion faculty from the School of Art took part in the process.

[15] The title today is Dean.

[16] "A Statement by the Jury," in the preface to *The 24th Biennial Exhibition* (Washington, DC: Corcoran Gallery of Art, 1955), unpaginated. Jurors for that Biennial were Hermann W. Williams, Jr., Philip R. Adams, James S. Plaut, and Andrew Carnduff Ritchie.

[17] Edward Hopper had been, and would continue to be, a regular participant in the Biennial as well as a juror.

[18] *The 30th Biennial Exhibition of Contemporary American Painting* (Washington, DC: Corcoran Gallery of Art, 1967), p. 5.

[19] Deed of Gift, May 10, 1869 CGSA Archives.

[20] Various graphic designs for the catalogues were used from the 1st Biennial (1907) through the 5th Biennial (1914). The longest string of consistency in both size and graphic design is found in the catalogues from the 6th Biennial (1916–1917) to the 20th Biennial (1947). A slightly larger format and design

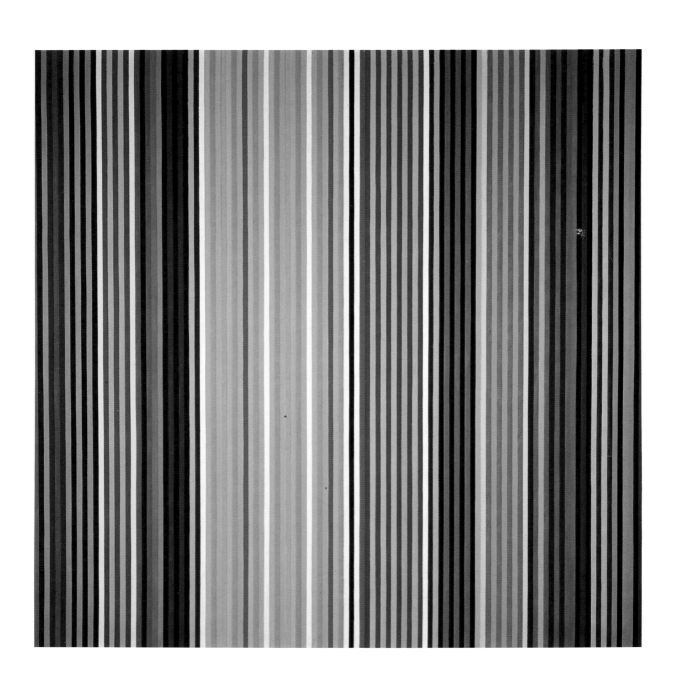

were used in the catalogues from the 21st (1949) through the 28th Biennial (1963). All subsequent Biennial catalogues have varied in size and design.

[21] The catalogue for the 20th Biennial (1947) was the first not to list all previous prize winners. Entries were listed in alphabetical order, and no index with addresses appeared at the back of this or any subsequent catalogue.

[22] Copies of only a few pamphlets survive in the CGSA Archives. Dated issues suggest they were published for the 4th Biennial (1912–13) through the 13th Biennial (1932–33).

[23] Files in the CGSA Archives do not include installation views before 1916. The most complete set of photographs for an early Biennial is from the 11th held in 1928.

[24] Paul Richard, *Washington Post,* 2 February 1969.

[25] The Rotunda is a round room designed by Charles Platt at the head of the grand staircase from the Atrium. It is on an intermediate level between the first and second floors. The second Biennial work created for this space was painted by Gene Davis for the 34th Biennial (1975).

[26] Senator from Montana, art collector and Trustee of the Corcoran Gallery of Art from 1914 to 1925.

[27] Washington businessman and Trustee of the Corcoran Gallery of Art from 1887 to 1936.

[28] Washington businessman and art dealer and Trustee of the Corcoran Gallery of Art from 1907 to 1911.

[29] This work, like many others in the exhibition has been returned to its original freshness and sound condition following treatment by Corcoran Conservator, Dare Hartwell, and her associates. I also thank her for her observation about the frequency of snow scenes and her other insights into paintings from the Biennials.

[30] Weber was not included again until the 12th Biennial of 1930–31.

[31] Stella was in the 19th Biennial (1945), one year before his death. MacDonald-Wright was in the 22nd Biennial (1951). O'Keeffe was in the 26th Biennial (1959).

[32] Press reaction to Rush's painting *The Broken Pitcher* in the 14th Biennial of 1935 indicates that the painting, probably an early attempt at abstraction, was not received well. It was described in the press as "fragments of a broken pitcher falling dizzingly down the entire length of the canvas assuming proportions that they would in the minds of those who might be unfortunate enough to break the picture."

[33] The exhibition needs of Washington artists were addressed in 1946 with the institution of the exhibition series *Work by Artists of Washington and Vicinity.* Informally known as the "area show" this series of juried shows was held irregularly on alternate years with the Biennial until the last one devoted to video took place in 1982.

[34] *New York Times,* 1 April 1952.

[35] Hermann Warner Williams, Jr., "Preface," *The 24th Biennial Exhibition* (Washington, DC: Corcoran Gallery of Art, 1955), unpaginated.

[36] Andrew Carnduff Ritchie, Philip R. Adams, and James S. Plaut, "A Statement by the Jury," *The 24th Biennial Exhibition* (Washington, DC: Corcoran Gallery of Art, 1955), unpaginated.

[37] Hermann Warner Williams, Jr., "Fifty Years of Biennial Exhibitions," *The 25th Biennial Exhibition* (Washington, DC: Corcoran Gallery of Art, 1957), p. 5.

[38] Ibid., p. 7.

[39] Foreword of *The 26th Biennial Exhibition* (Washington, DC: Corcoran Gallery of Art, 1959), unpaginated.

[40] Ibid.

[41] Hermann Warner Williams, Jr., "Fifty Years of Biennial Exhibitions," *The 25th Biennial Exhibition* (Washington, DC: Corcoran Gallery of Art, 1957), p. 5.

GENE DAVIS
(1920–1985)

Black Popcorn, 1965

Oil on canvas
Museum Purchase and exchange

THE 30TH BIENNIAL

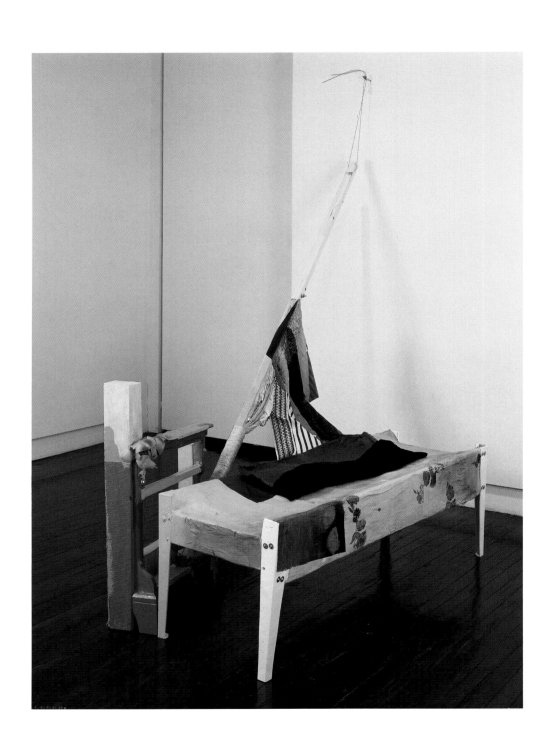

Terrie Sultan, Curator of Contemporary Art

Time has also changed the entire concept of the Biennial. Whereas in the early years of the century a broad survey, reasonably comprehensive and fair, of the artistic production of the entire country was possible to assemble, because to all intents and purposes all artists of any importance were located in a narrow band from Washington to Boston, this no longer holds true. For many years now it has been entirely beyond the capacity of any institution to demonstrate such a cross-section on a national scale, since painting of importance is being produced in all sections of the country.

— Hermann Warner Williams [1]

Biennials presented from 1969 to 1995 mirrored the fast-paced changes that were then affecting the contemporary art world. In retrospect, those Biennials also provide glimpses of the Corcoran's institutional challenge to come to terms with the emergence of new professional museum practices throughout the United States, as well as with increased institutional competition on the Washington museum scene.[2] From 1907 to 1968 just three directors had overseen the Corcoran. By contrast, ten changes in leadership occurred from 1969 to 1995; four of these took place from 1969 to 1975. The Biennial, perhaps the largest and most nationally visible of Corcoran curatorial projects, was seen by each new director as a highly desirable arena in which to introduce a personal aesthetic statement.

The Biennials of this period also reflected changing attitudes in American museums about the character and value of survey shows, and the general usefulness of such enterprises. As well, they called into question the specific capacity of these exhibitions to present a meaningful and comprehensive overview of current aesthetic discourse, which by 1970 had become increasingly diverse, divergent, and fractured along ideological and philosophical lines. The single biggest change in the Corcoran's attitude toward the Biennial was the assertion—repeated in every single catalogue foreword or essay published since 1969—that these exhibitions were no longer to be regarded as true surveys of American painting. The Biennials thus became curatorially driven exhibitions with a point of view, a singular aesthetic, or a unifying theme or idea, instead of being more objective overviews. Accompanying publications became more interpretive and educational, with the organizers using their essays as vehicles to develop ideas or to instruct the reading public. Quite unlike the pre-1969 projects that had presented the work of hundreds of artists, nine of the fourteen exhibitions held from 1969 to 1995 offered in-depth views—almost mini-solo exhibitions—of each participating artist. As

59

Jessica Stockholder
(b. 1959)

1994, 1994

Plastic sink legs, clothing, trimming, string, yarn, wood, hardware, piece of furniture, papier mâché, plaster, wallpaper paste, glue, and plastic fruit
Gift of the Women's Committee of the Corcoran Gallery of Art
The 44th Biennial

expenses incurred in organizing the modern Biennials increased, the Gallery sought to expand private, foundation, and corporate support. In addition to the Anna E. Clark Fund, established in 1927 to support the Biennial, the Morris and Gwendolyn Cafritz Foundation contributed to four Biennials during this period. By 1975 the National Endowment for the Arts began to support the exhibition regularly, and it continued to provide substantial funding for most Biennials for the next sixteen years.[3]

The 31st Biennial, presented in 1969 by the Corcoran's newly appointed director James Harithas, broadly signaled the change in the tone, direction, and organizational process that would govern subsequent Biennials. Invitational sections, which had been an integral part of the exhibitions beginning in 1915, had expanded to the point where, by 1965, invited artists comprised the majority of the exhibition.[4] Harithas formally declared the era of the juried Biennial over. Taking full responsibility for selecting all participants, he also reconfigured the selection format, effectively creating twenty-three separate solo exhibitions stationed throughout the museum. While different in process, this Biennial nevertheless continued to focus on and to reaffirm the hegemony of abstract color painting, which remained a strong regional force, even though the exhibition included no Washington artists. Harithas concentrated primarily on "younger artists living in New York who had not exhibited together, and had rarely been seen in a museum context, and artists who have made a significant contribution to American painting in the past and have received too little recognition." His primary intent was to present "various approaches to abstract paintings, each work representing a particular cosmological insight; also a transition from geometric abstraction to new expressionism."[5]

Although many of the artworks were selected from the artists' studios, Angelo Savelli and James Van Dijk created sited work in the Corcoran's galleries. The exhibition also included some surprises, such as neon wall pieces by Bruce Nauman, dyed canvas hangings by Richard Tuttle, and Savelli's three-dimensional sculpture. Juxtaposed with more well-known abstract painters like Larry Poons and Dan Christensen, Nauman, (who would become one of America's most innovative and celebrated artists) is barely mentioned in any of the reviews, which favored the lyric abstractionists. Hilton Kramer's response in the *New York Times* is typical: "Perhaps the most startling thing about this exhibition is not what it contains but what is does not. With one exception, there is not a trace of Pop art nor of its allied manifestations. The emphasis here is all on pure abstraction, both in its geometrical and its lyric forms."[6]

The Circumnavigation of the Sphering of the Poles (1964) by Irene Pereira was one of five works acquired from the exhibition. This painting, which shows Pereira at the peak of her creativity, is a classic mix of expressive brushstrokes and hard-edge geometry. She uses these two seemingly contradictory approaches to deftly allude to landscape through an interplay of geometric forms that seem to float away from an atmospheric field. This work dovetails in the Corcoran collection with earlier abstract paintings by Hans Hoffman, Josef Albers, and Mark Rothko, allowing the Gallery to present, in-depth, one of the highly refined approaches to postwar abstract painting. Along with the Pereira, Dean Fleming's *Atlantis*, Richard Tuttle's *Red Canvas*, Michael Goldberg's *Untitled*, and Robert Swain's *Untitled* were also added to the collection. These works reflected the overall theme of the exhibition, and firmly declared abstraction as a major focus for the Corcoran's modern and contemporary holdings.

IRENE RICE PEREIRA
(1907–1971)

The Circumnavigation of the Sphering of the Poles, 1964
Oil on canvas
Gift of the Associates of the Corcoran Gallery of Art
THE 31ST BIENNIAL

61

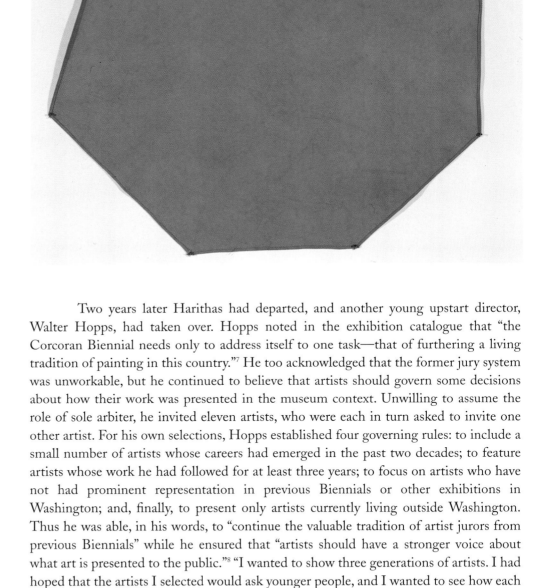

Two years later Harithas had departed, and another young upstart director, Walter Hopps, had taken over. Hopps noted in the exhibition catalogue that "the Corcoran Biennial needs only to address itself to one task—that of furthering a living tradition of painting in this country."[7] He too acknowledged that the former jury system was unworkable, but he continued to believe that artists should govern some decisions about how their work was presented in the museum context. Unwilling to assume the role of sole arbiter, he invited eleven artists, who were each in turn asked to invite one other artist. For his own selections, Hopps established four governing rules: to include a small number of artists whose careers had emerged in the past two decades; to feature artists whose work he had followed for at least three years; to focus on artists who have not had prominent representation in previous Biennials or other exhibitions in Washington; and, finally, to present only artists currently living outside Washington. Thus he was able, in his words, to "continue the valuable tradition of artist jurors from previous Biennials" while he ensured that "artists should have a stronger voice about what art is presented to the public."[8] "I wanted to show three generations of artists. I had hoped that the artists I selected would ask younger people, and I wanted to see how each would reinforce the other," Hopps recalled. "It was very surprising what happened. For example, instead of a young, emerging artist, Frank Lobdell selected Clyfford Still. He said he couldn't think of any other artist better for the show."[9]

Hopps presented a greater range of art than Harithas had, including figurative works. This selection largely countered the still dominant color-field painting that

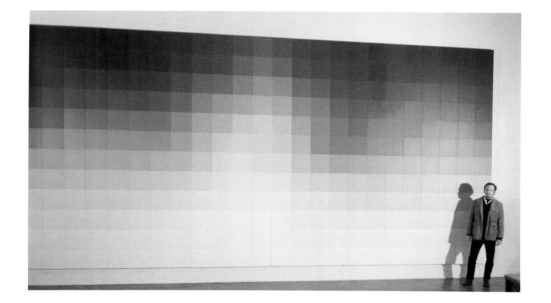

ROBERT SWAIN
(B. 1940)

Untitled, No 7, 1968–69

Installation view with
the artist, 1969
Acrylic on canvas
Gift of Mary Howland
Chase and the Friends
of the Corcoran Gallery
of Art

THE 31ST BIENNIAL

Harithas had reinforced in his exhibition. Like Harithas's project, however, the 32nd Biennial presented in 1971 consisted of a series of one-person shows within the context of an overall thematic exhibition. The press response to Hopps's endeavor was generally favorable. *Washington Post* critic Paul Richard proclaimed that Hopps "has revealed— with clarity—the vitality and chaos of contemporary painting."[10] In *Newsweek*, Douglas Davis pointed out some of the controversy Hopps's methods provoked locally. "Privately Hopps's critics charge him with shirking his 'personal curatorial responsibility.' To which he replies with great heat, 'Nonsense! Half the artists in the show are close personal friends of mine. I'm admitting that. Most of what passes for expertise in the art world, anyway, is personal involvement.'"[11] Considering that for decades Biennials were selected by a jury of working artists, criticism of Hopps's intentions to continue to engage the artists in the selection process seems a bit specious. Several women artists had another criticism worth noting: of the twenty-two artists presented, all were men. This occasioned Mary Beth Edelson, who was teaching at the Corcoran School of Art at the time, to organize a picket line during the opening. Hopps emphatically supports his contribution. "I think the Biennial was one of the half-dozen most interesting shows I organized for the Corcoran," he recently remarked.[12]

Three paintings came into the collection from the 32nd Biennial: *Teec* (1970) by Edward Moses, *Mandan, No. 19* (1970) by Franklin Owen, and *Reclining Nude on Green Couch* (1971) by Philip Pearlstein. Hopps had been forceful in the inclusion of representational work in the exhibition, and the acquisition of *Reclining Nude* significantly

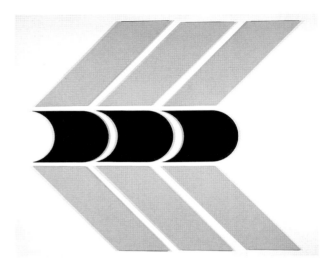

evolved the Gallery's already strong holdings of historical and modern figurative painting. In *Reclining Nude,* Pearlstein extends the tradition of the painted figure by shifting the traditional frontal focus of an odalisque, creating a dynamic, aggressive composition wherein the body literally pushes at the edges of the picture plane.

Gene Baro, the Corcoran's director from April to December 1972, was invited back in 1973 by acting director Roy Slade to express his opinion about American painting for the 33rd Biennial.[13] Reflecting his highly personal tastes, Baro returned to the theme of color abstraction and titled the exhibition *The Way of Color.* Seeking to establish a counter-reaction to the "happy accident" of the pour, stain, and geometry of color-field paintings, Baro focused on artists who were "attached to the best art of the recent past, a broad spectrum of solutions for colorism." All, he wrote, were involved in a "purposeful, controlled treatment of the surface."[14] This focus on color was well received by critics such as Benjamin Forgey of the *Washington Star,* who noted that Baro avoided the big names of the day, focusing instead on the "strength of the tradition" of color abstraction.[15] The Gallery's complex and largely unresolved relationship with artists living and working in Washington (who were then the primary practitioners of color-field painting outside New York) was exacerbated by the fact that none of these painters was invited to participate in Baro's Biennial. Rather, works by artists such as Thomas Downing and Gene Davis were installed in a separate exhibition in the downstairs galleries, a move that admittedly provided an interesting compare-and-contrast opportunity but effectively ghettoized the efforts of local artists. Even this was seen to be positive. "The extra dividend to the show is the opportunity to compare these paintings with works by Washington painters whose principal concern is color," Forgey wrote. "That, after all, is the game that gave this city its art name, and it's still the most active game in town." Baro's show is a "forth-right, honest, intelligible statement, and it engages the mind and heart. One could hardly ask for more."[16] However well regarded Baro's effort may have been locally, it was ignored by the national press.

It was perhaps due to the Gallery's institutional upheavals that no painting from this exhibition was acquired for the collection until late 1974, when private collectors donated Morteza Sazegar's *C5-72 #1* (1972).[17] Sazegar's optically active, painterly color-

PHILIP PEARLSTEIN
(B. 1924)

Reclining Nude on Green Couch, 1971

Oil on canvas

Gift of the Friends of the
Corcoran Gallery of Art

THE 32ND BIENNIAL

square combinations are inspired by colors in nature, and are indebted to Ellsworth Kelly's early pivotal abstraction, *Spectrum Colors Arranged by Chance* (1951–53). Darkly luminous, *C5-72 #1* is a sophisticated study of the inherent subtleties of color and hue.

    Roy Slade solidified and asserted his transition from acting to full director and retained the good will that Gene Baro's previous Biennial had engendered by offering Baro the role of advisor for the 34th Biennial in 1975. Significantly, Slade departed from in-depth selections. He invited fifty artists, but he allowed them to show only one work apiece. Broader in scope and yet smaller in scale, the 34th Biennial presented breadth at the expense of depth. "I was very excited about this project," Slade related. "We were on the verge of the Bicentennial, and I wanted to create a celebration of painting. I was excited to mix up East- and West-Coast artists, emerging and mature artists, and I was especially thrilled to introduce so many artists from California to an East-Coast audience for the first time."[18] Slade's catalogue essay was a rhapsodic ode to painting as represented in this diverse and purposefully unfocused exhibition, which featured repeat appearances from previous Biennials by half of the invited artists. This pause from the innovations introduced by Harithas and Hopps was both a crowd-pleaser and a critical success, with Paul Richard noting in the *Washington Post*, "It has been a while since the Corcoran offered an exhibition so ambitious and expensive."[19] In fact, Slade's resources to stage this Biennial had grown substantially. The previous Biennial was presented with a modest budget of $16,000; this exhibition was amply supported by more than $80,000 in grants.

TOP:
MORTEZA SAZEGAR
(B. 1933)

C5-72 #1, 1972

Acrylic on canvas
Gift of Mr. and Mrs. Gilbert
H. Kinney
THE 33RD BIENNIAL

BOTTOM:
FRANKLIN OWEN
(B. 1939)

Mandan, No. 19, 1970

Acrylic on canvas
Gift of the Friends of the
Corcoran Gallery of Art
THE 32ND BIENNIAL

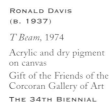
Of the fifty paintings included in the exhibition, the Corcoran acquired two. *T Beam* (1974) by Ronald Davis and *Creek Square* (1974) by Joan Synder are excellent examples of the differences intrinsic to East-Coast and West-Coast abstract painting, and their acquisition underscored Slade's stated desire to trace this difference in the exhibition. Davis's *T Beam* blends high-key, lyric, color-field atmospherics with exacting geometry, creating a visually complex hybrid of retinal and illusionistic gestural painting, and hard-edge definition. Monumentally scaled, *T Beam* deftly demonstrates the preoccupation with scale and light that then dominated the lexicon of California-based painters. Snyder's *Creek Square,* on the other hand, is relatively small in scale, but offers a densely packed, highly expressive study in color and motion. Snyder's roots in the New York School of Abstract Expressionism can be seen in her gooey, paint-laden brushstrokes and solid blocks of color. Theatrically placed as gestures on the surface of the picture plane, they create a heightened sense of emotional power and physical immediacy.

In 1977, Jane Livingston arrived as chief curator, a position she held for the next twelve years. The 35th Biennial, jointly organized by Livingston and Slade that year, again focused on abstract painting, but notably the curators looked beyond New York and selected from a much broader geographical base. Emphasizing yet again that the Biennial "does not attempt to survey or define the national scene, being instead the personal and considered choice of the Director and Chief Curator,"[20] the organizers sought to show that abstract painting in the 1970s remained deeply rooted in postwar Abstract Expressionism and represented what could be broadly defined as an American tradition. In pursuing this tradition, the curators consciously relegated realism and what they termed other "substyles" to the margins. "There were two main things Jane and I tried

to achieve in this Biennial," Slade recently explained. "One was to make sure that the Washington artists, people who had been previously shown only in the 'Washington room,' were mainstreamed. Secondly, after the criticism Hopps received, [we wanted] to make sure we included women."[21] Critical reception was mixed. Benjamin Forgey of the *Washington Star* acknowledged that the exhibition tried to make a point about significant art existing outside New York and other art centers, but he added, "Well, okay, but the show really tells us more about the Slade-Livingston taste than anything else. . . . So, we have a biennial that attempts no big statements, contains no striking new ideas, misses variety and lacks an aesthetic high point—an unmemorable, unassuming show. The virtue in this modesty . . . is that we are spared inflated notions about the state of the art and left peacefully alone to discover what we think of what Slade-Livingston uncovered for us."[22]

The broad national scope of this Biennial is reflected in the works that came into the collection from the exhibition. Washington artist Michael Clark had exhibited in many previous group shows at the Corcoran, and was the subject of a solo exhibition in 1971. His painting, *San Francisco Chinatown Windows* (1976), is an intimately scaled abstraction extrapolating geometry from daily life. In his investigation of spatial relationships, Clark uses observation as a pretext for abstraction, reducing the image of a window to a purely formal association of color and line. Frederick Hammersley, an established but underrecognized New Mexico-based artist, is largely known for his hard-edged painting of the early 60s, and the minimal, boldly geometric *Refer Two* (1973) is an excellent example of his work. Sandi Slone, now residing in New York, was an emerging artist based in Boston at the time of the exhibition. *Shivernly* (1976) was just recent-

JOAN SNYDER (B. 1940)

Creek Square, 1974

Oil, acrylic, canvas, cheesecloth, papier mâché on canvas

Gift of Marvin and Florence Gerstin

THE 34TH BIENNIAL

FREDERICK HAMMERSLEY
(B. 1919)

Refer Two, 1973–74

Oil on linen

Museum Purchase,
William A. Clark Fund

THE 35TH BIENNIAL

70

MICHAEL CLARK
(B. 1946)

San Francisco Chinatown Window, 1976

Oil on linen

Gift of the Friends of the
Corcoran Gallery of Art

THE 35TH BIENNIAL

ly added to the collection through a gift from a private collector. Unlike Clark and Hammersley, Slone's approach to abstraction is all gesture. *Shivernly's* muted tones of blended paint and broad brushstrokes are insistently its form and content.

Livingston assumed sole responsibility for the next two Biennials in 1979 and 1981, both of which focused narrowly on new work by five highly renowned painters. All male, all fifty years of age or older, the artists of the 36th Biennial, Jasper Johns, Willem de Kooning, Ellsworth Kelly, Robert Rauschenberg, and Roy Lichtenstein, had shown in previous ones and were selected, Livingston wrote in the catalogue, because they "are not only continuing to produce paintings in a spirit of refinement or elaboration of their own earlier achievements, but are making bodies of work which almost exceed in mastery, ambitiousness and sophistication much of their own earlier output."[23] She concluded her remarks by asserting that these artists were "making the best paintings of the time." The press mainly agreed, with Benjamin Forgey noting that "Livingston played it safe in this one, and came up a winner; and the least that can be said is that a winner is just what the Corcoran needs in its embattled competition with the awesome Mall museums."[24] Perhaps Forgey's positive comparison with the productions of the "awesome Mall museums" had an effect, because the 37th Biennial continued the same theme. Livingston basically renounced the idea of a national exhibition, having already declared her preference for a tightly focused presentation of a selective vision. Significantly, the five artists presented in 1981 included two women: Agnes Martin and Joan Mitchell. "These two Biennials represented a superlative moment in

SANDI SLONE (B. 1939)
Shivernly, 1976
Acrylic on canvas
Gift of Bruce L. Ehrmann
THE 35TH BIENNIAL

JOAN MITCHELL
(1926–1992)

Salut Tom, 1979

Oil on canvas

Museum Purchase with
aid of funds from the
Women's Committee of
the Corcoran Gallery of
Art and the National
Endowment for the Arts

THE 37TH BIENNIAL

American art, a moment that that might not ever be repeated," Livingston recently reminisced. "Everything is too pluralistic now. There was a clarity to those shows that Biennials don't usually have."[25]

The Gallery's high regard for the ten artists featured in these two exhibitions is reflected by their strong presence in the permanent collection. Richard Diebenkorn, Frank Stella, and Ellsworth Kelly were already represented by significant paintings in the collection prior to 1979. Joan Mitchell's *Salut Tom* (1979) also entered the collection in 1979, two years prior to the 37th Biennial (this painting was one of six major canvases representing Mitchell). A second-generation Abstract Expressionist, Mitchell relocated from New York to France in the 1950s. Her paintings, created with loose brushstrokes that, infused with the luminescent natural light of a bright white background, take on the quality of musical notation. Mitchell's aesthetic is more in tune with Monet's late grandly scaled *Waterlilies* than with her Abstract Expressionist predecessors, such as Jackson Pollock. *Salut Tom*, dedicated to American critic and curator Thomas Hess, is a signature work, a four-paneled panoramic composition that succinctly encapsulates the artist's personal, particularly lyrical perspective on the tradition of landscape-inspired abstraction.

Another radical alteration of the Biennial tradition occurred in 1983, when the project acquired a regional focus largely due to financial need. The Gallery, looking for new ways to support the heavy expense of researching and mounting a major survey exhibition, sought operating partners to share the fiscal burden. A regional approach also suited both the tenor of the times and the needs of corporate funders. Joining forces with the Western States Arts Foundation, the Corcoran presented the 38th Biennial as an extension of the Western States Biennial, a project begun by the Foundation in 1979 expressly to give Western artists national exposure. The following three Biennials addressed other regions of the United States: the Midwest in 1985; New York City in 1987; and the Southeast in 1989. Along with extra funding, the regional focus allowed a broader audience to enjoy these presentations, because for the first time in Biennial history, the works traveled to other museums and art centers within the specific regions addressed by the exhibition.

The 38th Corcoran Biennial/Second Western States Exhibition of 1983 was selected by a modified jury system, with the organizers soliciting nominations from artists and art experts from fourteen Western states. Slides of works by several hundred painters were reviewed by a curatorial committee comprised of Jane Livingston, Clair List, the Corcoran's associate curator of contemporary art, Linda Cathcart, curator of the Contemporary Art Museum in Houston, and George Neubert, curator of the San Francisco Museum of Modern Art. After the committee had reviewed slides and made preliminary selections, List visited studios to select specific works by each artist. In her essay, List noted that her selection "conveys the mystique of the Old West coupled with imagery from the New West; a sense of unashamed freedom to raid art history, folk art and both popular and frontier culture to fashion individualistic styles; a wry, satirical, even quirky storytelling; and throughout, the individual's response to the celebrated natural beauty of the West. . . ."[26] After an eight-year domination of purely abstract painting, this Biennial included a fair share of figuratively based, narrative work from diverse sources. The exhibition brought to the surface many opinions concerning the relevance of region-

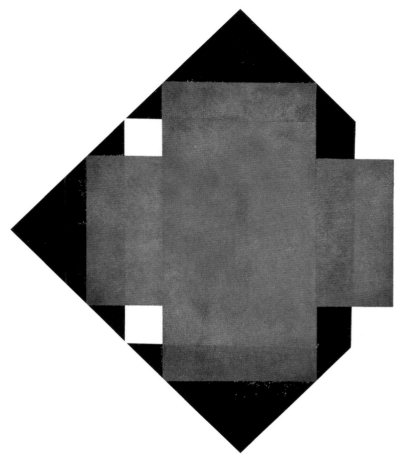

HARVEY QUAYTMAN
(B. 1937)

Age of Iron, 1986

Acrylic, rust, and collage
on canvas
Gift of the Friends of the
Corcoran Gallery of Art

THE 40TH BIENNIAL

SEAN SCULLY (B. 1945)

Flyer, 1986

Oil on canvas
Gift of the Women's
Committee of the Corcoran
Gallery of Art in memory
of Jinx Cutts with aid of
funds from the Firestone
Foundation and the Jinx
Cutts Memorial Fund

THE 40TH BIENNIAL

ROBERT MANGOLD
(B. 1937)

*Five Color Frame
Painting,* 1985

Acrylic on canvas

Gift of the Women's
Committee of the
Corcoran Gallery of Art

THE 40TH BIENNIAL

alism in contemporary art. "It is clear that western-based artists create under influences more complex than the quality of light on the desert or the patterns of Indian designs," critic Lee Fleming wrote in *ArtNews*. "The Western States exhibitions were founded to make this point: the Corcoran catalogue almost defeats it in a muddled attempt to restore something just short of provincialism to the word 'western.' This problem will only spread with future Corcoran Biennials if curators insist on tying regional art to geographic stereotypes."[27] The *New York Times* also weighed in with the assessment that "the notion of returning to the concept of 'regional' art seems disturbingly provincial."[28]

This same regional theme, which was then dominating national discourse, was strongly represented in the 39th Biennial, selected this time by independent guest curator Lisa Lyons. She reinstituted the role of being sole proprietor of the selection process. Her exhibition, which focused on the Midwestern states, sought to reveal "a gratifying reality: good painting, fresh and accomplished and inventive work, flourishes in all parts of our country. The slow process of the decentralization of the culture which has been underway for the past few decades is reaching a demonstrable maturity."[29] Lyons's approach to regionalism—that, in fact, regional distinctions no longer existed in the best contemporary art—occasioned a lengthy and impassioned refutation by Chicago critic Michael Bonesteel. Writing for *Art in America*, Bonesteel contended that "Lyons's assumption echoes what proponents of the bandwagon cosmopolitan view have been saying for years. . . . It is undeniable that regional distinctions are further diminishing with every generation. But to sound the death knell on Midwestern regionalism is at best

L. C. ARMSTRONG
(B. 1954)

Re-Coil, 1990

Enamel, fuse burn and
resin on three steel panels
Gift of the Women's
Committee of the
Corcoran Gallery of Art
THE 42ND BIENNIAL

premature. There's still some life—some independent life, that is—in the old provinces yet."[30] Unlike the East Coast critics who addressed the regionalism of the Western States Biennial as a negative move toward provincialism, Bonesteel reacted negatively toward what he saw as Lyons's attempt to differentiate between a geographic and a stylistic region on the basis of aesthetics.

Ned Rifkin assumed the position of curator of contemporary art at the Corcoran in 1985. He joined the Hirshhorn Museum and Sculpture Garden in 1987, and the 40th Biennial presented that year was his last project at the Gallery. Rifkin chose New York City as his regional focus, returning to an all-abstract painting show that purposefully reemphasized New York's primacy by declaring it the nation's capital of visual art. When asked to select his geographic region, Rifkin responded that "the only American geographic area that I believed was still genuinely 'regional' in the sense that it generated its own aesthetic and looked emphatically to itself and its own traditions, was New York City."[31] Rifkin, who had witnessed the strong emergence of neo-expressionist painting in the late 1980s, chose instead to focus on artists who he felt had "come through the 'crisis years' of painting" in the late 1960s and early 1970s, artists who he described as "midlife crisis artists." This approach was well received in Washington, with Paul Richard taking the lead in the *Washington Post* by declaring, "[Rifkin] picked no sharp, chic kids (the youngest is 37), and no 'blue chip' biggies (the oldest is 51). His exhibition, though a New York show, is not what you'd expect. It doesn't scuttle after fashion. . . . He left out those punky 'neo-expressionists' whose gloopy and aggressive dogs once howled through the East Village. He excluded the 'appropriationists' whose diffident, little borrowings tend to leave the viewer with the feeling he's been gypped."[32] Presenting thirteen participants

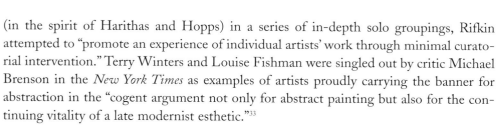

WILLY HEEKS (B. 1951)

Solace, 1990

Oil and charcoal on canvas
Gift of the Friends of the
Corcoran Gallery of Art
THE 42ND BIENNIAL

(in the spirit of Harithas and Hopps) in a series of in-depth solo groupings, Rifkin attempted to "promote an experience of individual artists' work through minimal curatorial intervention." Terry Winters and Louise Fishman were singled out by critic Michael Brenson in the *New York Times* as examples of artists proudly carrying the banner for abstraction in the "cogent argument not only for abstract painting but also for the continuing vitality of a late modernist esthetic."[33]

The final regional Biennial was presented in 1989. Organized by guest curator William Fagaly of the New Orleans Museum of Art, the 41st Biennial presented eighteen artists from the Southeast. Fagaly selected what he considered to be "talented painters who . . . have worked diligently and have not received the attention and recognition outside of the South they deserve,"[34] or emerging artists who also have not been recognized outside the South. He consciously avoided renowned artists such as Robert Rauschenberg and James Rosenquist, both of whom had already achieved international reputations. Two-thirds of the artists Fagaly selected worked in rural Southern communities and away from metropolitan centers; the rest lived in either Atlanta, Miami, or New Orleans. Almost all the works presented were image-based. The theme of narration generated some negative criticism, typified by Jane Addams Allen in the *Washington Times.* "Sadly, the overall look of the 41st Biennial suggests that the South is better adapted to literature than to art."[35] Nevertheless, exhibition organizer William Fagaly continues to feel that the Southern regional focus had merit. "I tried to show an eclectic mix—there was no 'look' to the show—to demonstrate the variety of techniques and approaches. . . . Mainly, I wanted to challenge the definition of painting by showing works as diverse as Dub Brock's paintings on bed sheets to Tyler Turkle's poured paint-

ings." He added, "I think that the idea of a regional exhibition is still viable. These shows help introduce artists who have not had much exposure. They give the artists, the ones who don't have established reputations, a validation of their work. Artists need that to continue, and if they don't get it, it impairs their output."[36] Jane Livingston agrees. "I think that the regional Biennials provided the artists with a real springboard from which to build careers. They were successful from the point of view of the artists, and that is really the only way to gauge success."[37]

Ironically, although the Corcoran was actively drawn to the national dialogue concerning regionalism in terms of exhibitions, the Gallery did not acquire works from any of its own regional biennials, with the notable exception of the 40th (New York City) Biennial. In addition to Sean Scully's *Flyer* (1986), acquired the year before the exhibition, *The Beach House* (1986) by Mary Heilmann, Harvey Quaytman's *Age of Iron* (1986), and *Five Color Frame Painting* (1985) by Robert Mangold were purchased from this show. Heilmann's painting compresses two-dimensional spatial relationships with a remarkable delicacy. Compositionally, *The Beach House* is a square within a rectangle, and the artist's loosely expressed brushwork and refined color activates the fundamentally planar nature of her composition. The minimalist geometry of Mangold's *Five Color Frame Painting,* part of a series of frame paintings begun in 1984, shows this artist opening up his pictorial construction, focusing on a center void framed by rectangles of harmonious color. Quaytman's *Age of Iron* also has a central image—this time a tilted cruciform—at its core. Like Mangold, Quaytman juxtaposes negative and positive spaces,

THOMAS ERIC STANTON
(B. 1947)

Tree of Life (Hannibal), 1991

Mixed media on canvas
Museum Purchase,
William A. Clark Fund
THE 42ND BIENNIAL

imbuing a purely visual abstraction with ambiguous spiritual content. Sean Scully's *Flyer* presents a more expressionistic, painterly surface, yet his architectural approach, which expands the picture plane into shallow relief, is also based on geometry. Taken together, these four paintings provide a consistent overview of the rigorous, sturdy, and durable New York abstraction of the middle 1980s.

In 1988, I joined the Gallery staff as curator of contemporary art. To counter eight years of regional programming, I proposed that the 42nd Biennial return to a national forum. Having had the luxury of time to research the overall trends in American painting for three years prior to the presentation of this Biennial in 1991, I proposed a series of exhibitions, each thematically focused on a single, important trend. In this scheme, the 42nd Biennial again returned to abstraction, while the 43rd featured figuration and the 44th Biennial presented works by artists who were exploring the boundaries of painting. Perhaps my biggest change was in redesigning the exhibition catalogues. In contrast to past efforts that generally included a single interpretive essay by the organizing curator, I invited outside critics and curators to contribute substantial catalogue entries on each artist.

In the wake of the Robert Mapplethorpe cancellation controversy of 1989, the 42nd Biennial was an opportunity for the Corcoran to project a national influence. Following the model of the 40th Biennial, this exhibition presented a series of thirteen small solo shows, with each artist assigned a gallery in which to present a relatively large number of works. Several of the artists planned their own installations specifically for the

allotted space. The overarching theme was to present works that "endow the formal eloquence of gestural and minimal abstraction with intellectual or emotional vigor,"[38] wherein a fusion of process, form, and content reinvigorates the painterly lexicon. The return to a national focus was well received, and the local critics' continuing dedication to abstract painting was evident. "The most urgent question facing painting at the moment—is it a viable artistic medium after more than a decade of mass-media derived art?—needs to be addressed in the broadest possible way," Eric Gibson wrote in the *Washington Times.*[39] The *Washington Post's* Paul Richard concurred, "Viewers who've been told that abstract painting is finished—that modernism is done, that oil paint and brushes are hopelessly antique—ought to see the '42nd Biennial Exhibition of Contemporary American Painting.' . . ."[40]

The paintings acquired from this exhibition offer prime examples of the two parallel concerns that informed abstraction in the 1990s: a cool, distanced style characterized by the use of industrial paints and materials that expands the minimalist tradition of painters such as Robert Mangold; and a naturally expressionistic, organic process that reconsiders Abstract Expressionism and the New York School. In *Re-Coil* (1990), L. C. Armstrong layers a highly fetishized, mirrored surface over a looped, expressionistic image (created by first arranging and then igniting dynamite fuse cord) that simulates the sensual gesture of a brushstroke. The result is a seductive dialogue between transparency and opacity, distance and emotion. Lydia Dona's *Fear of Falling into the Lack, The Dream of Language, and The Ruptures of the Flood* (1991), with its field of acid,

KIM DINGLE (B. 1951)

*Black Girl Dragging
White Girl*, 1992

Oil and charcoal on
canvas

Gift of the Women's
Committee of the
Corcoran Gallery of Art

THE 43RD BIENNIAL

CHARLES GARABEDIAN
(B. 1923)

Study for "The Iliad",
1992

Acrylic on paper
Gift of the Friends of the
Corcoran Gallery of Art

THE 43RD BIENNIAL

industrial, or unnatural color in agitated, overlapping drips and mechanized diagrams, illustrates a decidedly post-modern take on the primacy of the abstract gesture. For all their differences, both Willy Heeks and Thomas Eric Stanton represent a more consistently organic mode of abstraction. Heeks's luminous, sensual color is related to nineteenth-century sublime landscapes, as well as to the drip aesthetic of Jackson Pollock, and in *Solace* (1990) he synthesizes richly allusive images rooted in natural systems and archetypal forms. Thomas Stanton's *Tree of Life (Hannibal)* (1991) meshes multiple layers of thick paint to conceal personalized iconography based on natural models and personal memories. With his collection of quasi-representational images, numbering and patterning systems, and highly refined, hard-edged representation, Lari Pittman pushes image into abstraction. His *Reverential and Needy* (1991) envisions the dual impulses of nature and the manmade as a formal strategy to bridge the gap between abstraction and representation.

By 1993, issues of the body—both social and psychological—had emerged as a central topic throughout contemporary artistic practice, and the serial progression I had proposed in 1989 took on added urgency. Several museums had already presented exhibitions exploring this topic, but primarily through the lens of sculpture, film, and hybrid media, such as installation. Using the format of the Biennial as a natural venue in which to explore this issue via painting, the 43rd Biennial viewed the body not in the tradition of a still-life studio prop, but as a form freighted with provocative personal and social meaning. The twenty-three participants included a combination of mature, mid-career,

IDA APPLEBROOG
(B. 1929)

Mother mother I am ill,
1993

Oil on canvas
Museum Purchase,
the Jacob and Charlotte
Lehrman Foundation
Memorial Art Fund

THE 43RD BIENNIAL

and emerging artists. Representations by the first generation provided a fulcrum for meditations on a wide variety of social and political issues that had gained prominence in 1950s and 1960s, while the work of the second-generation artists who had achieved recognition in the 1970s and early 1980s, invoked both mythology and autobiography. Paintings by the younger, emerging artists demonstrated both influences, extending the boundaries of their medium while continuing to embrace the painted figure as the ultimate metaphor for the human condition. Focusing on the figure not only meant that the content of the works was equally important to the formal aspects that were precedent in abstract painting, but it also served as a significant departure from Biennial tradition. "Like many another exhibition in the 1990s," John Russell wrote in the *New York Times*, "this one touches on the prejudice, fear and racial hatred that beset millions of people all over the world. But it does not address those problems in the boilerplated and robotic way that is virtually mandatory elsewhere. This year's biennial is there to make us think them through afresh." He continued, "It is a brainy show, in which Homer, Flaubert and Freud can be alluded to without pretension. It has a breadth of reference, a gift for telling metaphor, a mischievous candor and a readiness to talk back to life."[41]

Because the 43rd Biennial was figurative in its theme, the Gallery was presented with a natural opportunity to add works to the collection that would continue the dialogue with the human body that had been an established part of the Corcoran's mandate since its inception. These artists demonstrate highly personalized responses to the challenge of painterly representation toward the end of the twentieth century. What sets their work apart from their forebears is their willingness to actively investigate, either overtly or covertly, a wide variety of social and political issues. Kim Dingle has been called a feminist with a sense of humor, and it is true that she uses girls in party dresses to diffuse any overt recognition of the anger and violence that dominates her imagery. Dingle's double portrait, *Black Girl Dragging White Girl* (1992), is expressed with a refreshing stylistic forthrightness that enhances the ambiguous social interaction depicted. Full of historic allusions and ironic humor, Charles Garabedian's interpretation of Homer's epic themes becomes a meditation on the foibles of 20th-century cultural development and technological advancement. The figures in his *Study for the Iliad* (1992) are, unlike Dingle's characters, positioned in an atmospheric, flatly rendered landscape. Painted with a luminous glow, they radiate a sense of timelessness. Ida Applebroog's people also inhabit unusual, otherworldly landscapes that are equal parts fantasy and reality. In *Mother mother I am ill* (1993), the picture plane is crowded with image snippets that kaleidoscope into an overall narrative, wherein the seemingly innocent children's fable is undercut by suggestions of violence and danger. The surface of the painting glistens with a rich, buttery medium; like the other figurative artists discussed here, the formal beauty of Applebroog's process underscores the complexity of her content.[42]

The last Biennial in this series, presented in 1995, was entitled *Painting Outside Painting*. Reinforcing the Corcoran's recognition that the definition of painting had changed, the works in this exhibition were dedicated to "reconceptualizing and refiguring the structure of painting."[43] Many of the artists presented work that incorporated aspects of sculpture or installation, emphasizing shapes as a means of translating the idea of the referential brushstroke into a three-dimensional entity; others used nontra-

FABIAN MARCACCIO
(B. 1963)

Paint-Zone #12, 1994–95
Collograph, oil on canvas
Promised gift of Anthony
T. Podesta

THE 44TH BIENNIAL

ditional painterly materials, such as perfume, knitting yarn, poisonous chemicals, rubber, or plaster. Several artists—Polly Apfelbaum, Sam Gilliam, Lauren Szold, and James Hyde—selected places throughout the museum for which to create site-specific works. In echoing the innovations of Harithas's sited works of the 31st Biennial in 1969, this brought the tradition full circle. Alternatively hailed as the "freshest, most relaxed and approachable biennial in years"[44] or an exhibition that reduces "the latest skirmishes at painting's borders to little more than stupid painting tricks,"[45] the 44th Biennial served as the coda to the Corcoran's almost ninety-year commitment to American painting.

Jessica Stockholder's *1994* is a prime example of a work of art that operates in the blurred boundary between painting and sculpture. *1994* is constructed like a three-dimensional Abstract Expressionist painting, as if the color and composition of a Hans Hoffman canvas had been crushed, extruded outward, and somehow taken solid form in the gallery. Stockholder employs a profusion of found objects, fabric, yarn, and other flotsam and jetsam of everyday life to make shapes and lines in space, creating physically dynamic compositions that use the vocabulary of painting to explore the concerns of space, volume, weight, and mass that are traditionally associated with sculpture. In *Paint-Zone #12,* Fabian Marcaccio isolates essential painterly actions, such as brushstrokes and drips, and reproduces or recombines them to create a "painting" that presents a unique take on the value of the individual gesture to the act of painting. Stuart Arends *O.S. 50* (1994) also investigates the relationship between color and form. This oil-on-steel painted cube, mounted flush to the wall, occupies a similarly blurred territory between painting and sculpture. These works offer a practical response to the theoretical deconstruction of traditional painting, and set the stage in the Gallery's collection for the next wave of painterly investigation.

What is the future of the Biennial? The Corcoran postponed the 45th Biennial—originally scheduled for 1997—before deciding to dedicate this exhibition to the permanent collection. That motivated Jo Ann Lewis of the *Washington Post* to pose the question, "After nearly a century of tracking the cutting edge in American painting, has the Corcoran Biennial become obsolete?"[46] The Gallery is currently reevaluating and reassessing the project. "We need to look at the point of biennials in the future," Deputy Director and Chief Curator Jack Cowart told Lewis. "Are they doing what they were doing, now that we have rapid communications and countless galleries, art magazines and newspaper reviews to keep us constantly apprised of new developments?" He concluded, "We want to find a way to make the biennial meaningful."[47]

The Biennials have not always been sites of innovation. Often they have served to confirm the prevailing tastes of the times or the specific preferences of the jurors or sole organizer. Certainly, many of our most renowned painters participated at one time or another, and scores of them are represented in the Corcoran's permanent collection. More than a few artists who are now highly regarded, however, did not participate in Biennials, including postwar Abstract Expressionists Barnett Newman, Mark Rothko, and Jackson Pollock. In more recent times, several artists now considered significant, such as Eric Fischl, Susan Rothenberg, David Salle, Julian Schnabel, and Donald Sultan, were not included. Based on my research and own personal experience, I would say that this disconnect between what is critically perceived as the established values of the moment and the exhibition curator's conceptual intention is deliberate. Such counter-

programming is generally motivated by the curator's desire to develop and promote a specific idea or theme.

My own opinion, seconded by several past Biennial organizers, is that this freedom to experiment and to take a risk in the service of an idea establishes and confirms the continued value of this kind of serial exhibition. My predecessors, however, offered a mixed response to the question of the enduring viability of the Biennial as it is currently structured. As early as 1969 James Harithas believed that the concept should be expanded to include diverse media and to reach beyond the United States. "My dream," he recounted, "was to include Canadian and South American artists, to make the Biennial really about the Americas. Now, you have to go international." Pointedly, he added, "I don't see how you can do a Biennial now without photography. Photographs are the way we reflect our universe."[48] By contrast, Roy Slade asserted, "The point is that painting has an extremely important place in our history. As a celebration of contemporary American painting, I think the Biennial has great validity and still fills a real need."[49] Lisa Lyons concurred. "I tend to be a fan of highly focused exhibitions," she admitted, "and with painting, there is something important and real to focus on."[50] As usual, Walter Hopps was succinct. "I'll take Norman Mailer's stance: 'It absolutely depends on the talent in the room.' "[51]

— T.S.

STUART ARENDS
(B. 1950)

O.S. 50, 1994

Oil on steel
Gift of the Artist
THE 44TH BIENNIAL

[1] Hermann Warner Williams, director of the Corcoran (1947–68), quoted by James Harithas in the foreword to *The 31st Biennial Exhibition of Contemporary American Painting* (Washington, DC: Corcoran Gallery of Art, 1969), unpaginated.

[2] Two obvious sources of competition were the Hirshhorn Museum and Sculpture Garden, established in 1974, and the East Wing of the National Gallery of Art, which opened in 1978.

[3] The Morris and Gwendolyn Cafritz Foundation supported Biennials in 1971, 1975, 1977, and 1979. The National Endowment for the Arts is acknowledged as a supporter of the 34th through 42nd Biennials (except the 38th Biennial).

[4] The Thirtieth Biennial was comprised of a total of forty-five participants, thirty-five of whom were invited.

[5] James Harithas, in the foreword of *The 31st Biennial Exhibition of Contemporary American Painting* (Washington, DC: Corcoran Gallery of Art, 1969), unpaginated.

[6] Hilton Kramer, "The Corcoran Biennial: Something Old, Something New," *New York Times,* 23 February 1969, D31.

[7] Walter Hopps, in the introduction to *The 32nd Biennial Exhibition of Contemporary American Painting* (Washington, DC: Corcoran Gallery of Art, 1971), 8.

[8] Ibid.

[9] Walter Hopps, telephone interview with the author, 30 March 1998.

[10] Paul Richard, "Corcoran's Suggestive Thought-Fields," *Washington Post,* 27 February 1971, C1.

[11] Douglas Davis, "Artists as Critics," *Newsweek,* 29 March 1971, 65.

[12] Walter Hopps, telephone interview with the author, 30 March 1998.

[13] Gene Baro, director, and Vincent Melzac, chief executive officer, were both relieved of their posts following a fistfight during the opening of an exhibition of paintings by Sam Francis on 2 November 1972. The announcement of their departure was published in the *Washington Post* on 1 December 1972.

[14] Gene Baro, in the introduction of the exhibition catalogue *The Way of Color: 33rd Biennial Exhibition of Contemporary American Painting* (Washington, DC: Corcoran Gallery of Art, 1973), unpaginated.

[15] Benjamin Forgey, "The Biennial: Color as Poetry," *Sunday Star and Daily News,* 25 February 1973, G1.

[16] Ibid.

[17] During the time the 33rd Biennial was on view, and for several months thereafter, the Corcoran underwent a number of significant institutional changes, including a restructuring of the Board of Trustees, a search for a new director, and the dismissal of the assistant curator of exhibitions.

[18] Roy Slade, telephone interview with the author, 9 April 1998.

[19] Paul Richard, "A Flashy, Festive Biennial," *Washington Post,* 21 February 1976, B1.

[20] Roy Slade, in the preface of *The 35th Biennial Exhibition of Contemporary American Painting* (Washington, DC: Corcoran Gallery of Art, 1977), 5.

[21] Roy Slade, telephone interview with the author, 10 April 1998.

[22] Benjamin Forgey, "Off-Center Paintings," *Washington Star,* 27 February 1977, H1.

[23] Jane Livingston, *The 36th Biennial Exhibition of Contemporary American Painting* (Washington, DC: Corcoran Gallery of Art, 1979), 45.

[24] Benjamin Forgey, "Stunning Art by New York's Finest," *Washington Star,* 25 February 1979, E1.

[25] Jane Livingston, telephone interview with the author, 30 March 1998.

[26] Clair List, in the introduction to *The 38th Biennial Exhibition of Contemporary American Painting/Second Western States Exhibition* (Washington, DC: Corcoran Gallery of Art, 1983), 10.

[27] Lee Fleming, "The Corcoran Biennial/Second Western States Exhibition," *ArtNews* (May 1983), 127–29.

[28] Grace Glueck, "Two Biennials: One Looking East and the Other West," *New York Times,* 27 March 1983, H35.

[29] Jane Livingston, in the introduction to *The 39th Biennial Exhibition of Contemporary American Painting* (Washington, DC: Corcoran Gallery of Art, 1985), 9.

[30] Michael Bonesteel, "The 39th Corcoran Biennial: The Death Knell of Regionalism?" *Art in America* (October 1985), 31–37.

[31] Ned Rifkin, in the introduction to *The 40th Biennial Exhibition of Contemporary American Painting* (Washington, DC: Corcoran Gallery of Art, 1987), 12.

[32] Paul Richard, "Painting in Past Tints," *Washington Post,* 11 April 1987, C1.

[33] Michael Brenson, "True Believers Who Keep the Flame of Painting," *New York Times,* 7 June 1987. Brenson pointed out that Fishman and Winters were also included in the Whitney Biennial, which was running concurrently in New York City.

[34] William Fagaley, *The 41st Biennial Exhibition of Contemporary American Painting* (Washington, DC: Corcoran Gallery of Art, 1989), 13.

[35] Jane Addams Allen, "Biennial Focuses on Southern Gothic," *Washington Times,* 5 April 1989, E1.

[36] William Fagaly, telephone interview with the author, 30 March 1998.

[37] Jane Livingston, telephone interview with the author, 30 March 1998.

[38] Terrie Sultan, "The Realm of Forms as the Object of Knowledge," *The 42nd Biennial Exhibition of Contemporary American Painting* (Washington, DC: Corcoran Gallery of Art, 1991), 15.

[39] Eric Gibson, "Corcoran puts painting to test as viable form," *Washington Times,* 6 September 1991.

[40] Paul Richard, "Abstract and Personal," *Washington Post,* 6 September 1991, F1.

[41] John Russell, "The Corcoran Gives New Meaning to 'Biennial,'" *New York Times,* 21 November 1993, 39.

[42] *Mother mother I am ill* was included in the 43rd Biennial under the title *Freida S.* The painting was subsequently retitled, and included in Applebroog's major survey exhibition *Ida Applebroog: Nothing Personal, Paintings, 1987–1997,* organized by the Corcoran and presented here March 14 through June 1, 1998. The painting was acquired by the Gallery in 1998.

[43] Terrie Sultan, "Painting Outside Painting," *The 44th Biennial Exhibition of Contemporary American Painting* (Washington, DC: Corcoran Gallery of Art, 1995), 17.

[44] Jo Ann Lewis, "Painting Outside the Lines," *Washington Post,* 23 December 1995, B1.

[45] Roberta Smith, "Testing Limits at the Corcoran," *New York Times,* 6 January 1996, B11.

[46] Jo Ann Lewis, "The Biennial, Exhibiting a Few Wrinkles," *Washington Post,* 10 July 1997, B1.

[47] Ibid.

[48] James Harithas, telephone interview with the author, 14 April 1998.

[49] Roy Slade, telephone interview with the author, 9 April 1998.

[50] Lisa Lyons, telephone interview with the author, 20 April 1998.

[51] Walter Hopps, telephone interview with the author, 30 March 1998.

ADDENDUM

Paige Turner, Assistant Curator of Exhibitions

*This addendum summarizes exhibition information for Biennials from 1969–1995,
the period covered in the preceding essay by Terrie Sultan.*

31ST EXHIBITION
*February 1–March 16, 1969
Organized by
James Harithas, Director*

34-page catalogue with introduction by James Harithas,
biographies, checklist

10 color, 25 b/w illustrations

78 works (all abstract),
22 artists (11 New York,
4 California, 7 elsewhere)

JO BAER
DARBY BANNARD
BEN BERNS
DAVID BUDD
DAN CHRISTENSEN
NASSOS DAPHNIS
RON DAVIS
DEAN FLEMING
MICHAEL GOLDBERG
TOM HOLLAND
LEE LOZANO
CLARK MURRAY
BRUCE NAUMAN
IRENE RICE PEREIRA
WILLIAM PETTET
LARRY POONS
ANGELO SAVELLI
MYRON STOUT
ROBERT SWAIN
RICHARD TUTTLE
JAMES VAN DIJK
PETER YOUNG

32RD EXHIBITION
*February 28–April 4, 1971
Organized by
Walter Hopps, Director*

80-page catalogue with introduction by Walter Hopps,
biographies, checklist

49 b/w illustrations

64 works (styles range from
geometric minimalism to figurative), 22 artists (10 New
York, 9 California, 3 elsewhere)

DIRECTOR SELECTION
RICHARD ESTES
SAM FRANCIS
ROBERT IRWIN
RICHARD JACKSON
ROY LICHTENSTEIN
FRANK LOBDELL
DAVID NOVROS
PHILIP PEARLSTEIN
EDWARD RUSCHA
PETER SAUL
DAVID STEPHENS

ARTIST SELECTION
PETER DEAN
ROBERT DURAN
JOE GOODE
ROBERT GORDON
ALEX KATZ
SIMMIE KNOX
EDWARD MOSES
FRANKLIN OWEN
CLYFFORD STILL
WAYNE THIEBAUD
JOSHUA YOUNG

33RD EXHIBITION
*February 24–April 8, 1973
Organized by
Gene Baro, Guest Curator*

30-page catalogue with
foreword by Roy Slade,
Director, introduction by
Baro, biographies, checklist

12 color illustrations,
12 b/w portraits of artists

110 works (all abstract),
12 artists (7 New York,
3 California, 2 elsewhere)

BILLY AL BENGSTON
SUSAN CRILE
ANTHONY DEBLASI
RICHARD DIEBENKORN
CRAIG KAUFFMAN
JANE KAUFMAN
DOUG OHLSON
MORTEZA SAZEGAR
ALBERT STADLER
PHILIP WOFFORD
ROBERT ZAKANYCH
KES ZAPKUS

34TH EXHIBITION
February 22–April 6, 1975
Organized by
Roy Slade, Director

120-page catalogue with introduction by Roy Slade, biographies, checklist

11 color, 43 b/w illustrations

50 works (abstract and representational styles), 50 artists (32 New York, 5 California, 5 Washington, DC, 8 elsewhere)

RICHARD ANUSZKIEWICZ
JENNIFER BARTLETT
JAKE BERTHOT
JAMES BROOKS
CHUCK CLOSE
WILLIAM CONLON
ALAN COTE
GENE DAVIS
RONALD DAVIS
WILLEM DE KOONING
RICHARD DIEBENKORN
WILLIAM DUTTERER
FRIEDEL DZUBAS
HELEN FRANKENTHALER
SAM GILLIAM
GRACE HARTIGAN
MICHAEL HEIZER
AL HELD
TOM HOLLAND
GARY HUDSON
ROBERT HUDSON
ROBERT INDIANA
TERENCE LA NOUE
MARILYN LENKOWSKY
SOL LEWITT
RICHARD LINDNER
ALVIN LOVING
JOAN MITCHELL
EDWARD MOSES
ROBERT MOTHERWELL
LOWELL NESBITT
KENNETH NOLAND
JULES OLITSKI
PHILIP PEARLSTEIN

LARRY POONS
DOROTHEA ROCKBURNE
LUDWIG SANDER
PAUL SARKISIAN
ALAN SHIELDS
JOAN SNYDER
STEVEN SORMAN
ALBERT STADLER
FRANK STELLA
ANN TRUITT
JACK TWORKOV
JOHN WALKER
ANDY WARHOL
TOM WESSELMANN
WILLIAM T. WILEY
PHILIP WOFFORD

35TH EXHIBITION
February 26–April 3, 1977
Organized by
Jane Livingston, Chief
Curator, and Roy Slade,
Director

80-page catalogue with preface by Roy Slade, interpretive essay by Jane Livingston (first interpretive essay by curator), biographies, checklist

15 color, 22 b/w illustrations

75 works (largely abstract), 24 artists (conscious effort to diversify: 4 New York, 6 California, 14 additional major art centers nationwide)

JOHN ALEXANDER
KARL BENJAMIN
PAUL BROWN
MICHAEL CLARK
MAX COLE
HERBERT CREECY
JEFF DAVIS
TONY DELAP
PAUL DILLON
MICHAEL GOLDBERG
FREDERICK HAMMERSLEY
DAVID HEADLEY
RAY HERDEGEN
DARRYL HUGHTO
O. W. "PAPPY" KITCHENS
ROGER KIZIK
MARTIN MYERS
LUCINDA PARKER
BASILIOS POULOS
GREGG RENFROW
SANDI SLONE
ALMA THOMAS
JIM WAID
ROBERT YASUDA

36TH EXHIBITION
February 24–April 8, 1979
Organized by
Jane Livingston, Chief
Curator

56-page catalogue with interpretive essay by Jane Livingston, essay by Linda Simmons, *A Brief History of The Corcoran Biennial 1907–1967*, biographies, checklist

30 color illustrations

30 works (all abstract), 5 artists (5 New York)

WILLEM DE KOONING
JASPER JOHNS
ELLSWORTH KELLY
ROY LICHTENSTEIN
ROBERT RAUSCHENBERG

37th Exhibition

February 19–April 5, 1981
Organized by
Jane Livingston, Chief
Curator

52-page catalogue with
interpretive essay by Jane
Livingston, one-line biography
for each artist, checklist

25 color, 8 b/w illustrations

28 works plus site-specific
pieces by Richard Serra
(all abstract), 5 artists (2 New
York, 1 California, 1 New
Mexico, 1 France)

RICHARD DIEBENKORN
AGNES MARTIN
JOAN MITCHELL
RICHARD SERRA
FRANK STELLA

38th Exhibition:

SECOND WESTERN STATES

February 3–April 3, 1983
Organized by Clair List,
Associate Curator of
Contemporary Art

93-page catalogue with preface
by Cheryl Alters and Bill
Jamison, Western States Arts
Foundation, introduction
by Jane Livingston, Chief
Curator, interpretive essay
by Clair List, biographies,
checklist

30 color illustrations, 106
works (abstract and representational styles), 30 artists (9
California, 21 other western
States)

TRAVELED TO: Lakeview
Museum of Arts and Sciences,
Peoria, Illinois; Scottsdale
Center for the Arts,
Scottsdale, Arizona;
Albuquerque Museum,
Albuquerque,
New Mexico; Long Beach
Museum of Art, Long Beach,
California; San Francisco
Museum of Modern Art,
San Francisco, California

PETER ALEXANDER
CHARLES ARNOLDI
JOE BAKER
WULF BARSCH
DAVID BATES
ED BLACKBURN
JOAN BROWN
JOHN E. BUCK
ROBERT COLESCOTT
JAMES G. DAVIS
LADDIE JOHN DILL
CHUCK DUGAN
JOHN FINCHER
VERNON FISHER
JOHN R. FUDGE
ALLAN GRAHAM

GAYLEN HANSEN
RON HOOVER
JAMES HUETER
ALDEN MASON
MICHAEL C. MCMILLEN
MARGARET NIELSEN
DAN RIZZIE
MICHELE RUSSO
RAYMOND SAUNDERS
JAUNE QUICK-TO-SEE SMITH
MASAMI TERAOKA
THEODORE J. WADDELL
R. LEE WHITE
DANNY WILLIAMS

39th Exhibition

February 2–April 7, 1985
Organized by
Lisa Lyons, Guest Curator

80-page catalogue with preface
by Michael Botwinick,
Director, introduction by
Jane Livingston, Chief
Curator, interpretive essay
by Lisa Lyons, artists' statements, biographies, checklist

80 works (abstract and representational styles), 17 artists (7
midwestern states)

TRAVELED TO: Mary and
Leigh Block Gallery,
Northwestern University,
Evanston, Illinois; Butler
Institute of American Art,
Youngstown, Ohio;
Contemporary Art Center,
Cincinnati, Ohio

NICHOLAS AFRICANO
MACYN BOLT
JOHN BROENEN
ROGER BROWN
PETER HUTTINGER
TOM KEESEE
LANCE KILAND
ROBERT LOSTUTTER
JIM LUTES
KAY MILLER
MICHAEL NAKONECZNY
DENNIS NECHVATAL
KEN NEVADOMI
JIM NUTT
ED PASCHKE
HOLLIS SIGLER
T. L. SOLIEN

40TH EXHIBITION

April 11– June 21, 1987
Organized by Ned Rifkin,
Curator of Contemporary Art

78-page catalogue with preface by Jane Livingston, Chief Curator, introduction and entries on each artist, by Ned Rifkin, artists' statements, biographies, checklist

13 color illustrations

86 works (all abstract), 13 artists (13 New York)

GREGORY AMENOFF
LOUISE FISHMAN
MARY HEILMANN
BILL JENSEN
JONATHAN LASKER
ROBERT MANGOLD
ELIZABETH MURRAY
HARVEY QUAYTMAN
DAVID REED
SEAN SCULLY
JOAN SNYDER
ANDREW SPENCE
TERRY WINTERS

41ST EXHIBITION

April 5–June 4, 1989
Organized by William Fagaly, Guest Curator and Assistant Director of the New Orleans Museum

64-page catalogue with introduction by Christina Orr-Cahall, Director, Corcoran Gallery of Art, interpretive essay by William Fagaly, biographies, checklist

18 color illustrations

82 works (mixture of abstract and representational), 18 artists (18 southeastern states)

TRAVELED TO: Georgia Museum of Art, Athens, Georgia; New Orleans Museum of Art, New Orleans, Louisiana; Norton Gallery and School of Art, West Palm Beach, Florida.

CARLOS ALFONZO
DUB BROCK
WARREN FARR
TINA GIROUARD
CHERYL GOLDSLEGER
JAMES HERBERT
MEDFORD JOHNSTON
J. B. MURRY
MICHAEL NORTHUIS
ART ROSENBAUM
MICHAEL SCOTT
STEVE SWEET
ROBERT THIELE
TYLER TURKLE
RUSS WARREN
ROBERT WARRENS
EDWARD WHITEMAN
DONALD ROLLER WILSON

42ND EXHIBITION

September 7–
November 10, 1991
Organized by Terrie Sultan, Curator of Contemporary Art

88-page catalogue with foreword by David C. Levy, Director, interpretive essay by Terrie Sultan, individual artist catalogue entries by Ken Johnson, Elizabeth McBride, Terry Myers, David Pagel, Maria Porges, biographies, checklist

13 color and 26 b/w illustrations

83 works (all abstract), 13 artists (7 New York, 4 California, 1 Washington, DC, 1 elsewhere)

L. C. ARMSTRONG
NANCY CHUNN
LYDIA DONA
WILLY HEEKS
TISHAN HSU
JUDY MANNARINO
MICHAEL MILLER
SABINA OTT
IRENE PIJOAN
LARI PITTMAN
ELDRIDGE RAWLS
THOMAS ERIC STANTON
ANDREA WAY

43RD EXHIBITION

October 30, 1993–
January 2, 1994
Organized by Terrie Sultan, Curator of Contemporary Art

112-page catalogue with foreword by Jack Cowart, Deputy Director and Chief Curator, interpretive essay by Terrie Sultan, individual artist catalogue entries by Maia Damianovic, Judith Russi Kirshner, Klaus Ottmann, David Pagel, Maria Porges, Marla Price, Gary Sangster, Lowery Stokes Sims, Alisa Tager, biographies, checklist

25 color, 24 b/w illustrations

91 works (all representational), 25 artists (9 New York, 8 California, 8 elsewhere)

IDA APPLEBROOG
KEN APTEKAR
DOTTY ATTIE
LUIS CRUZ AZACETA
DONALD BAECHLER
DREW BEATTIE
PHYLLIS BRAMSON
MICHAEL BYRON
CAROLE CAROOMPAS
ROBERT COLESCOTT
DANIEL DAVIDSON
KIM DINGLE
INGA FRICK
CHARLES GARABEDIAN
LEON GOLUB
CATHERINE HOWE
DAVID HUMPHREY
HUNG LIU
JIM LUTES
KERRY JAMES MARSHALL
MELISSA MILLER
MANUEL OCAMPO
DEBORAH OROPALLO
ELENA SISTO
NANCY SPERO

Measurements are in inches, height precedes width

WORKS ON VIEW IN
The Forty-fifth Biennial: The Corcoran Collects, 1907–1998
ARE INDICATED IN
COLOR

FIRST ANNUAL EXHIBITION: OIL PAINTINGS BY CONTEMPORARY AMERICAN ARTISTS
February 7 – March 9, 1907

EDWIN AUSTIN ABBEY (1852–1911)
Sylvia, 1899–1900
Oil on canvas
48 ⅛ x 48 ⅛
William A. Clark Collection 26.1

THOMAS ANSHUTZ (1851–1912)
A Dutchman
Oil on canvas
80 ½ x 40 ½
Gift of Mrs. Louise Bennett 15.2
Deaccessioned in 1957

RALPH ALBERT BLAKELOCK (1847–1919)
Moonlight, c. 1890
Oil on canvas
27 ¹/₁₆ x 37 ¹/₁₆
William A. Clark Collection 26.8
Part of Senator William Clark Bequest
to Corcoran Gallery of Art in 1925

GEORGE BOGERT (1864–1944)
Sunset
Oil on canvas
27 ½ x 36
Gift of George A. Hearn
Deaccessioned in 1962

MARY STEVENSON CASSATT (1844–1926)
Woman and Child
Oil on canvas
27 x 22 ½
Museum Purchase 07.25
Returned to artist's dealer in 1909 as partial
payment for *Susan on a Balcony Holding a Dog*
(2nd Exhibition)

PAUL DOUGHERTY (1877–1947)
The Land and the Sea, 1906
Oil on canvas
36 ⅛ x 48 ¹/₁₆
Museum purchase, Gallery Fund 07.5

ALBERT LOREY GROLL (1866–1952)
The Land of the Hopi Indian
Oil on canvas
50 ½ x 39 ½
Museum Purchase 07.26
Returned to artist in 1911 in partial payment for
No-Man's Land, Arizona (3rd Exhibition)

CHILDE HASSAM (1859–1935)
Northeast Headlands – New England Coast, 1901
Oil on canvas
25 x 30
Museum Purchase, Gallery Fund 07.8

WINSLOW HOMER (1836–1910)
A Light on the Sea, 1897
Oil on canvas
28 ¼ x 48 ¹/₁₆
Museum Purchase, Gallery Fund 07.3

GARI MELCHERS
Edward C. Walker, c. 1906

ALBERT LOREY GROLL
No-Man's Land, Arizona, before 1910

WILTON LOCKWOOD (1861–1914)
Peonies
Oil on canvas
29 ½ x 29 ½
Museum Purchase 07.6
Deaccessioned in 1957

GARI MELCHERS (1860–1932)
Edward C. Walker, c. 1906
Oil on canvas
54 ⅛ x 40 ⅞
Bequest of Edward C. and Mary Walker 37.34

WILLARD LEROY METCALF (1858–1925)
May Night, 1906
Oil on canvas
39 ¼ x 36 ³/₁₆
Museum Purchase, Gallery Fund 07.7
First William A. Clark Prize and
Corcoran Gold Medal

EDWARD WILLIS REDFIELD (1869–1965)
The Delaware River
Oil on canvas
31 ¼ x 40
Museum Purchase 07.24
Returned to artist in 1924 as partial payment
for *The Mill in Winter* (9th Exhibition).

JAMES JEBUSA SHANNON (1862–1923)
Girl in Brown, 1907
Oil on canvas
43 ⅛ x 33 ⅛
Museum Purchase, Gallery Fund 07.1

ROSWELL SHURTLEFF (1835–1915)
The First Snow
Oil on canvas
30 x 40 ⅛
Museum Purchase 07.2
Deaccessioned in 1948

JAMES DAVID SMILLIE (1833–1909)
The Cliffs of Normandy, 1885
Oil on canvas
41 ½ x 66 ½
Museum Purchase, Gallery Fund 07.10

WILLIAM THORNE (1864–1956)
The Terrace
Oil on canvas
41 ¼ x 27 ¼
Museum Purchase 07.9
Deaccessioned in 1960

HORATIO WALKER (1858–1938)
Ave Maria
Oil on canvas
46 ¼ x 34 ¼
Museum Purchase 07.4
Deaccessioned in 1955

SECOND EXHIBITION: OIL PAINTINGS BY CONTEMPORARY AMERICAN ARTISTS
December 8, 1908 – January 17, 1909

MARY STEVENSON CASSATT (1844–1926)
Susan on a Balcony Holding a Dog, c. 1880
Oil on canvas
39 ½ x 25 ½
Museum Purchase, Gallery Fund 09.8

WILLIAM KENDALL (1869–1938)
Narcissa
Oil on canvas
51 x 30
Museum Purchase 09.4
Deaccessioned in 1948

ROBERT LEE MacCAMERON (1866–1912)
Groupe d'Amis, 1907
Oil on canvas
51 ⅛ x 65
Museum Purchase, Gallery Fund 09.9

WALTER MacEWEN (1860–1943)
An Ancestor
Oil on canvas
74 x 33 ½
Museum Purchase 09.3
Deaccessioned in 1951

LEONARD OCHTMAN (1854–1934)
November Morning
Oil on canvas
30 ⅛ x 40 ⅛
Museum Purchase 09.7
Deaccessioned in 1957

CHARLES PEARCE (1851–1914)
Bergère
Oil on canvas
29 x 24
Gift of Mrs. Walter MacEwen 28.4
Deaccessioned in 1962

ROBERT REID (1862–1929)
The Open Fire, 1908
Oil on canvas
44 ½ x 42 ¼
Museum Purchase 09.5
Third William A. Clark Prize and
Corcoran Bronze Medal
Deaccessioned in 1951

ELMER SCHOFIELD (1867–1944)
Morning after Snow
Oil on canvas
38 x 48
Museum Purchase 09.6
Returned to artist in 1922 as partial
payment for *Cliff Shadows* (8th Exhibition)

EDMUND CHARLES TARBELL (1862–1938)
Josephine and Mercie, 1908
Oil on canvas
28 ⅛ x 32 ¼
Museum Purchase, Gallery Fund 09.2

THIRD EXHIBITION: OIL PAINTINGS BY CONTEMPORARY AMERICAN ARTISTS
December 10, 1910 – January 22, 1911

BEN FOSTER (1852–1926)
Sunset in the Litchfield Hills, c. 1910
Oil on canvas
30 ¼ x 36 ⅛
Museum Purchase, Gallery Fund 11.4

DANIEL GARBER (1880–1958)
April Landscape, before 1910
Oil on canvas
42 ¹/₁₆ x 46 ¹/₁₆
Museum Purchase, Gallery Fund 11.2
Fourth William A. Clark Prize and
Corcoran Honorable Mention Certificate

ALBERT LOREY GROLL (1866–1952)
No-Man's Land, Arizona, before 1910
Oil on canvas
40 ¼ x 51 ⅜
Museum Purchase, Gallery Fund 11.7

GARI MELCHERS (1860–1932)
The Smithy, 1910
Oil on canvas
57 ⅛ x 51 ½
Gift of Duncan Phillips 50.10

GARI MELCHERS (1860–1932)
Penelope, 1910
Oil on canvas
54 ½ x 50 ⅞
Museum Purchase, Gallery Fund 11.1
Second William A. Clark Prize and
Corcoran Silver Medal

CHARLES REIFFEL (1862–1942)
Railway Yards-Winter Evening, c. 1910
Oil on canvas
18 ⅛ x 24 ³/₁₆
Museum Purchase, Gallery Fund 11.6

GEORGE SYMONS (1863–1930)
Snow Clouds
Oil on canvas
56 x 63
Museum Purchase 11.5
Returned to artist in 1929 as partial payment for
Where Long Shadows Lie (7th Exhibition)

IRVING RAMSAY WILES (1861–1948)
The Student, 1910
Oil on canvas
30 ⅜ x 25
Museum Purchase, Gallery Fund 11.3

IRVING RAMSAY WILES
The Student, 1910

FRANK WESTON BENSON
My Daughter, 1912

FOURTH EXHIBITION: OIL PAINTINGS BY CONTEMPORARY AMERICAN ARTISTS
December 17, 1912 – January 26, 1913

FRANK WESTON BENSON (1862–1951)
My Daughter, 1912
Oil on canvas
30 ¼ x 25 ¼
Museum Purchase, Gallery Fund 12.8

RICHARD NORRIS BROOKE (1847–1920)
Incoming Tide, 1912
Oil on canvas
25 x 38
Museum Purchase 12.7
Deaccessioned in 1942

JOHN FABIAN CARLSON (1875–1945)
Woods in Winter, before 1912
Oil on canvas
46 ⅛ x 56 ⅛
Museum Purchase, Gallery Fund 12.5

BEN FOSTER (1852–1926)
Late Autumn Moonrise, before 1912
Oil on canvas
42 x 48
Museum Purchase 12.6
Deaccessioned in 1951

CHILDE HASSAM (1859–1935)
The New York Window, 1912
Oil on canvas
45 ⅞ x 35
Museum Purchase, Gallery Fund 12.10
First William A. Clark Prize and Corcoran
Gold Medal

CHAUNCEY FOSTER RYDER (1868–1949)
Cape Porpoise, before 1912
Oil on canvas
32 x 40
Museum Purchase, Gallery Fund 12.9

JULIAN ALDEN WEIR (1852–1919)
Autumn, 1906
Oil on canvas
36 x 28 ⅞
Museum Purchase, Gallery Fund 12.4

FIFTH EXHIBITION: OIL PAINTINGS BY CONTEMPORARY AMERICAN ARTISTS
December 15, 1914 – January 24, 1915

BRUCE CRANE (1857–1937)
November Hillsides
Oil on canvas
32 x 40
Museum Purchase 14.4
Deaccessioned in 1959

RICHARD FARLEY (1875–1954)
Fog, 1914
Oil on canvas
39 ½ x 57 ½
Museum Purchase 14.6
Fourth William A. Clark Prize and Corcoran
Honorable Mention Certificate
Deaccessioned in 1959

PHILIP HALE (1865–1931)
Portrait – Girl with Muff, before 1914
Oil on canvas
30 ⅜ x 25 ¼
Museum Purchase 14.5

JOHN FABIAN CARLSON
Woods in Winter, before 1912

JULIAN ALDEN WEIR
Autumn, 1906

BIRGE HARRISON (1854–1929)
Rose and Silver – Moonrise
Pastel
29 ½ x 39 ½
Museum purchase 14.10
Deaccessioned in 1925

GARI MELCHERS (1860–1932)
Maternity, c. 1913
Oil on canvas
63 x 43
Museum Purchase, Gallery Fund 19.2

J. CAMPBELL PHILLIPS (1873–1949)
The First Born
Oil on canvas
36 ¼ x 30
Museum Purchase 14.2
Deaccessioned in 1957

EDWARD WILLIS REDFIELD (1869–1965)
Sleighing, 1914
Oil on canvas
36 x 30
Museum Purchase 14.11
Returned to artist in 1924 as partial payment
for *The Mill in Winter* (9th Exhibition)

JOHN SINGER SARGENT (1856–1925)
Simplon Pass, 1911
Oil on canvas
28 ¼ x 36 ½
Bequest of James Parmelee 41.22

HELEN TURNER (1858–1958)
Girl With a Lantern, 1914
Oil on canvas
44 x 34
Museum Purchase 14.3
Deaccessioned in 1957

JULIAN ALDEN WEIR (1852–1919)
Portrait of Miss de L., 1914
Oil on canvas
30 3/16 x 25
Museum Purchase, Gallery Fund 14.7
First William A. Clark Prize and
Corcoran Gold Medal

**SIXTH EXHIBITION: OIL PAINTINGS BY
CONTEMPORARY AMERICAN ARTISTS**
December 17, 1916 – January 21, 1917

DINES CARLSEN (1901–1966)
The Brass Kettle, 1916
Oil on canvas
20 ¼ x 24 ¼
Museum Purchase, Gallery Fund 16.6

EMIL CARLSEN (1853–1932)
Moonlight on a Calm Sea, 1915–1916
Oil on canvas
58 ¼ x 47 ¼
Museum Purchase, Gallery Fund 16.7

WILLIAM MERRITT CHASE (1849–1916)
William Andrews Clark, c. 1915
Oil on canvas
50 1/16 x 40 1/8
Gift of William Andrews Clark 17.3

GARI MELCHERS
Maternity, c. 1913

DINES CARLSEN
The Brass Kettle, 1916

JOSEPH RODEFER DECAMP (1858–1923)
The Seamstress, 1916
Oil on canvas
36 ¼ x 28 ¼
Museum Purchase, Gallery Fund 16.4

SIDNEY DICKINSON (1890–1978)
Portrait of the Artist, 1915
Oil on canvas
34 ¼ x 24 ¼
Museum Purchase, Gallery Fund 16.5

ERNEST LAWSON (1873–1939)
Boathouse, Winter, Harlem River, 1916
Oil on canvas
40 ⅜ x 50
Museum Purchase, Gallery Fund 16.3
Second William A. Clark Prize and
Corcoran Silver Medal

HAYLEY LEVER (1876–1958)
Dawn, before 1916
Oil on canvas
50 ¼ x 60 ¼
Museum Purchase, Gallery Fund 16.8

WILLIAM PAXTON (1869–1941)
The House Maid, 1910
Oil on canvas
30 ¼ x 25 ⅛
Museum Purchase, Gallery Fund 16.9

ROBERT REID (1862–1929)
The Japanese Screen
Oil on canvas
37 ¼ x 30
Museum Purchase 16.2
Deaccessioned in 1957

JOHN SINGER SARGENT (1856–1925)
Mrs. Henry White, 1883
Oil on canvas
87 x 55
Gift of Mr. John Campbell White 49.4

EDMUND CHARLES TARBELL (1862–1938)
Josephine Knitting, 1916
Oil on canvas
26 ⅛ x 20 ³⁄₁₆
Bequest of George M. Oyster, Jr. 24.2

CHARLES YOUNG (1869–1964)
The North Wind, 1915
Oil on canvas
30 ⅜ x 40 ⅝
Museum Purchase 17.1
Deaccessioned 1962

**SEVENTH EXHIBITION: OIL PAINTINGS
BY CONTEMPORARY AMERICAN ARTISTS**
December 21, 1919 – January 25, 1920

FREDERIC BARTLETT (1873–1953)
Canton Street, 1919
Oil on canvas
36 ¼ x 40 ½
Museum Purchase, Gallery Fund 19.28

FRANK WESTON BENSON (1862–1951)
The Open Window, 1917
Oil on canvas
52 ⅛ x 42 ⅛
Museum Purchase 19.30
First William A. Clark Prize and
Corcoran Gold Medal

SIDNEY DICKINSON
Portrait of the Artist, 1915

EDMUND CHARLES TARBELL
Josephine Knitting, 1916

FREDERICK FRIESEKE (1874–1939)
Lady in Pink, 1918
Oil on canvas
32 x 32
Museum Purchase 19.35
Returned to artist in 1921 as partial payment
for *Peace* (8th Exhibition)

CHILDE HASSAM (1859–1935)
Old House at Easthampton, 1916
Oil on canvas
32 ⅜ x 39 ⅝
Bequest of George M. Oyster, Jr. 24.6

ROBERT HENRI (1865–1929)
Willie Gee
Oil on canvas
32 x 36
Museum Purchase 19.35
Returned to artist in 1924 as partial payment
for *Indian Girl in White Ceremonial Blanket*
(9th Exhibition)

FELICIE HOWELL (1897–1968)
A New England Street, 1918
Oil on canvas
30 x 40
Museum Purchase 19.33
Deaccessioned in 1962

JOHN MURPHY (1853–1921)
Landscape, 1898
Oil on canvas
24 ⅛ x 36 ⅛
William A. Clark Collection 26.147

BERTHA PERRIE (1868–1921)
In Gloucester Harbor, 1919
Oil on canvas
20 x 40
Museum Purchase 19.32
Deaccessioned in 1953

CHARLES PLATT (1861–1933)
Early Autumn
Oil on canvas
33 x 36
Bequest of James Parmelee 41.55
Deaccessioned in 1957

EDWARD ROOK (1870–1960)
Peonies
Oil on canvas
30 x 36
Museum Purchase 19.31
Third William A. Clark Prize and Corcoran
Bronze Medal
Deaccessioned in 1957

ROBERT SPENCER (1879–1931)
The Red Boat, before 1919
Oil on canvas
30 ⅛ x 36 ¼
Museum Purchase 19.29

GEORGE SYMONS (1863–1930)
Where Long Shadows Lie (also *Where Waters Flow
and Long Shadows Lie*), before 1919
Oil on canvas
50 ¼ x 60 ¼
Museum Purchase, Gallery Fund 19.27

JULIAN ALDEN WEIR (1852–1919)
Obweebetuck, c. 1908
Oil on canvas
24 ⅛ x 33 ¾
Bequest of George M. Oyster, Jr. 24.3

CHARLES WOODBURY (1864–1940)
Monadnock, 1912
Oil on canvas
36 ³⁄₁₆ x 48 ³⁄₁₆
Museum Purchase, Gallery Fund 19.36

**EIGHTH EXHIBITION: OIL PAINTINGS
BY CONTEMPORARY AMERICAN ARTISTS**
December 18, 1921 – January 22, 1922

SAMUEL BURTIS BAKER (1882–1967)
Interior with Figure, 1920
Oil on canvas
50 ¹⁄₁₆ x 40 ½
Museum Purchase, William A. Clark Fund 36.1
Second William A. Clark Prize and Corcoran Silver Medal

EMIL CARLSEN (1853–1932)
The White Jug, c. 1919
Oil on canvas
25 ¼ x 30
Gift of Mrs. Emil Carlsen and Dines Carlsen 35.12

JOHN FOLINSBEE (1892–1972)
Gray Thaw, c. 1920
Oil on canvas
32 ¼ x 40 ½
Museum Purchase, Gallery Fund 21.7

FREDERICK FRIESEKE (1874–1939)
Peace, 1917
Oil on canvas
40 ½ x 60 ⅛
Museum Purchase, Gallery Fund 21.8

DANIEL GARBER (1880–1958)
South Room – Green Street, 1921
Oil on canvas
50 ⁹⁄₁₆ x 42 ¼
Museum Purchase, Gallery Fund 21.6
First William A. Clark Prize and
Corcoran Gold Medal

EDWARD WILLIS REDFIELD (1869–1965)
Overlooking the Valley, c. 1921
Oil on canvas
38 x 50 ¼
Bequest of George M. Oyster, Jr. 24.7

ELMER SCHOFIELD (1867–1944)
Cliff Shadows, 1921
Oil on canvas
50 x 60 ⅛
Museum Purchase, Gallery Fund 21.9

WALTER UFER (1876–1936)
Strange Things
Oil on canvas
40 x 36
Museum Purchase 21.42
Returned to artist in 1924 as partial payment
for *Sleep* (9th Exhibition)

FREDERIC BARTLETT
Canton Street, 1919

ROBERT SPENCER
The Red Boat, before 1919

CHARLES WOODBURY
Monadnock, 1912

EMIL CARLSEN
The White Jug, c. 1919

THE NINTH EXHIBITION OF CONTEMPORARY AMERICAN OIL PAINTINGS
December 16, 1923 – January 20, 1924

CECILIA BEAUX (1863–1942)
Sita and Sarita, c. 1921
Oil on canvas
36 ⅞ x 25 ⅛
Museum Purchase, William A. Clark Fund 23.4

LOUIS BETTS (1873–1961)
Yvonne, c. 1922
Oil on canvas
24 ⅛ x 18 ⅛
Gift of Louis Betts 39.6

CATHARINE CRITCHER (1876–1968)
Light Lightning, 1923
Oil on canvas
30 x 25
Museum Purchase, William A. Clark Fund 23.5
Deaccessioned in 1960

FREDERICK FRIESEKE (1874–1939)
Dressing Room, 1922
Oil on canvas
25 ½ x 31 ¾
Museum Purchase, Gallery Fund 23.6

LILLIAN WESTCOTT HALE (1881–1963)
Eleanor
Oil on canvas
30 ½ x 22 ½
Museum Purchase 23.7
Deaccessioned in 1977

GEORGE HALLOWELL (1871–1926)
Wissataquoik River Drive, c. 1920
Oil on canvas
25 ¼ x 30 ¼
Museum Purchase, William A. Clark Fund 23.8

CHARLES HAWTHORNE (1872–1930)
The Fisherman's Daughter, c. 1912
Oil on wood panel
60 x 48
Museum Purchase, Gallery Fund 23.16

ROBERT HENRI (1865–1929)
Indian Girl in White Ceremonial Blanket, c. 1921
Oil on canvas
32 x 26
Museum Purchase, Gallery Fund 23.15

JOHN JOHANSEN (1876–1964)
Portrait of the Artist's Family, 1922
Oil on canvas
30 x 40
Museum Purchase 23.18
Returned to artist in 1926 as partial payment for
The Artist and His Family (10th Exhibition)

MAURICE PRENDERGAST (1859–1924)
Landscape with Figures, 1921
Oil on canvas
32 ⅝ x 42 ½
Museum Purchase, William A. Clark Fund 23.17
Third William A. Clark Prize and
Corcoran Bronze Medal

EDWARD WILLIS REDFIELD
Overlooking the Valley, c. 1921

FREDERICK FRIESEKE
Dressing Room, 1922

EDWARD WILLIS REDFIELD (1869–1965)
The Mill in Winter, 1922
Oil on canvas
50 ³/₁₆ x 56 ⁵/₁₆
Museum Purchase, Gallery Fund 23.11

LEOPOLD SEYFFERT (1887–1956)
John C. Johnson, 1921
Oil on canvas
30 ¼ x 25 ¼
Museum Purchase, William A. Clark Fund 23.12

HENRY TYLER (1855–1931)
Late Afternoon
Oil on canvas
20 ¼ x 24 ⅜
Museum Purchase, William A. Clark Fund 23.13
Deaccessioned in 1957

WALTER UFER (1876–1936)
Sleep
Oil on canvas
50 x 50
Museum Purchase 23.14
Deaccessioned in 1961

**THE TENTH EXHIBITION OF
CONTEMPORARY AMERICAN OIL
PAINTINGS**
April 4 – May 16, 1926

FRANK WESTON BENSON (1862–1951)
Still Life, 1925
Oil on canvas
32 ¹/₁₆ x 40
Museum Purchase, William A. Clark Fund 26.802

EMIL CARLSEN (1853–1932)
The Picture from Thibet, c. 1920
Oil on canvas
38 ⅜ x 27 ¼
Bequest of James Parmelee 41.3

JOHN JOHANSEN (1876–1964)
The Artist and His Family, 1925
Oil on canvas
30 x 40
Museum Purchase, William A. Clark Fund 26.799

LEOPOLD SEYFFERT (1887–1956)
Myself, 1925
Oil on composition board
27 x 24
Museum Purchase, William A. Clark Fund 26.801

ROBERT VONNOH (1858–1933)
Self Portrait, 1920
Oil on canvas
22 x 18
Bequest of Bessie Potter Vonnoh Keyes 55.69

**THE ELEVENTH EXHIBITION OF
CONTEMPORARY AMEICAN OIL
PAINTINGS**
October 28 – December 9, 1928

ARTHUR BOWEN DAVIES (1862–1928)
Stars and Dews and Dreams of Night, 1927
Oil on canvas
40 x 26
Museum Purchase, William A. Clark Fund 28.7

JOHN JOHANSEN
The Artist and His Family, 1925

LEOPOLD SEYFFERT
Myself, 1925

ROBERT VONNOH
Self Portrait, 1920

ARTHUR BOWEN DAVIES (1862–1928)
The Umbrian Mountains, 1925
Oil on canvas
25 ⅞ x 39 ⅞
Museum Purchase, William A. Clark Fund 28.8

DANIEL GARBER (1880–1958)
The Sycamore
Oil on canvas
[dimensions unknown]
Bequest of James Parmelee 41.44
Returned to artist in 1944 in exchange for 26
works on paper

BERNARD KARFIOL (1886–1952)
Summer, 1927
Oil on canvas
46 ⅜ x 60 ⅜
Museum Purchase, William A. Clark Fund 28.6
First William A. Clark Prize and
Corcoran Gold Medal

JONAS LIE (1880–1940)
The Storm, c. 1925
Oil on canvas
30 ⅛ x 45
Museum Purchase, William A. Clark Fund 26.800

HENRY MCFEE (1886–1953)
The Window
Oil on canvas
24 x 20
Museum Purchase 28.9
Returned to artist in 1937 as partial payment
for *Corner of a Room* (15th Exhibition)

**THE TWELFTH EXHIBITION OF
CONTEMPORARY AMERICAN OIL
PAINTINGS**
November 30, 1930 – January 11, 1931

BRYSON BURROUGHS (1869–1934)
Demeter and Persephone, 1917
Oil on canvas
36 ⅛ x 24 1/16
Museum Purchase, William A. Clark Fund 30.7

JOHN GRABACH (1886–1981)
River Barges
Oil on canvas
36 x 42 1/16
Museum Purchase 30.6
Returned to artist in 1941 in exchange for *Waterfront*

JOHN NOBLE (1874–1934)
Early Morning, before 1930
Oil on composition board
16 x 19 ½
Museum Purchase, William A. Clark Fund 30.8

EUGENE SPEICHER (1883–1962)
Sara Rivers, 1924
Oil on canvas
45 ¾ x 37
Museum Purchase, William A. Clark Fund 30.9

MAURICE STERNE (1878–1957)
After Lunch, 1930
Oil on composition board
29 x 39
Museum Purchase, William A. Clark Fund 30.5
First William A. Clark Prize and Corcoran
Gold Medal

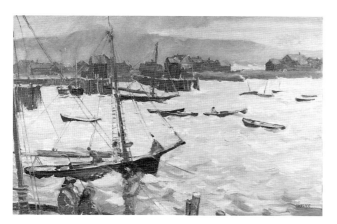

JONAS LIE
The Storm, c. 1925

BRYSON BURROUGHS
Demeter and Persephone, 1917

THE THIRTEENTH EXHIBITION OF CONTEMPORARY AMERICAN OIL PAINTINGS
December 4, 1932 – January 15, 1933

ALEXANDER BROOK (1898–1980)
Peggy Bacon (formerly *My Wife*), 1932
Oil on canvas
34 ¹/₁₆ x 26
Museum Purchase, Gallery Fund 32.12

ROCKWELL KENT (1882–1971)
Adirondacks, 1928–30
Oil on canvas
38 ⅜ x 54 ⅜
Museum Purchase, William A. Clark Fund 34.4

GEORGE LUKS (1867–1933)
Woman with Black Cat, 1932
Oil on canvas
30 ⅜ x 25 ⅜
Museum Purchase, Gallery Fund 32.13
First William A. Clark Prize and
Corcoran Gold Medal

PEPPINO MANGRAVITE (1896–1978)
Family Portrait, 1930
Oil on canvas
24 ¼ x 30 ¼
Museum Purchase, Gallery Fund 32.10

JEROME MYERS (1867–1940)
Life on the East Side, 1931
Oil on canvas
30 ⅛ x 40 ⅛
Museum Purchase, Gallery Fund 32.11

DAVID SILVETTE (B. 1909)
Thornton Nye of Wytheville, 1931
Oil on canvas
77 x 37
Museum Purchase, Gallery Fund 32.8
Third William A. Clark Prize and Corcoran
Bronze Medal

JOHN SLOAN (1871–1951)
Yeats at Petitpas, 1910
Oil on canvas
26 x 32
Museum Purchase, Gallery Fund 32.9

THE FOURTEENTH BIENNIAL EXHIBITION OF CONTEMPORARY AMERICAN OIL PAINTINGS
March 24 – May 5, 1935

JULIUS BLOCH (1888–1966)
The Striker
Oil on canvas
54 ¼ x 40 ¼
Museum Purchase, Anna E. Clark Fund 35.11
Deaccessioned in 1962

JOHN CONNER (1869–1945)
Saint Francis
Oil on canvas
30 ⅛ x 25 ¼
Museum Purchase, Anna E. Clark Fund 35.5
Deaccessioned in 1957

109

JOHN NOBLE
Early Morning, before 1930

EUGENE SPEICHER
Sara Rivers, 1924

RANDALL DAVEY (1887–1964)
Paddock No. 1, c. 1931
Oil on canvas
20 ¼ x 30 ¼
Museum Purchase, Anna E. Clark Fund 35.6

LAUREN FORD (1891–1981)
Choir Practice, 1934
Oil on panel
13 ¾ x 18 ⅛
Museum Purchase, Anna E. Clark Fund 35.7

RICHARD MILLER (1875–1943)
Torso
Oil on composition board
36 ¼ x 39 ⅞
Museum Purchase 35.10
Deaccessioned in 1957

ROSS MOFFETT (1888–1971)
Provincetown Wharf, c. 1935
Oil on canvas
30 ¼ x 42 ¼
Museum Purchase, Anna E. Clark Fund 35.8

JOHN THOMPSON (1882–1945)
Still Life – Rubber Plant, 1935
Oil on canvas
30 ⅜ x 36 ½
Museum Purchase, Anna E. Clark Fund 35.9
Deaccessioned in 1951

EUGEN WEISZ (1890–1954)
Self-Portrait, 1935
Oil on canvas
21 ¹⁄₁₆ x 15 ⅛
Museum Purchase, Anna E. Clark Fund 43.14

THE FIFTEENTH BIENNIAL EXHIBITION OF CONTEMPORARY AMERICAN OIL PAINTINGS
March 28 – May 9, 1937

GEORGE BIDDLE (1885–1973)
Helene Sardeau, 1931
Oil on canvas
25 ¼ x 35 ¼
Gift of the Artist 68.33.5

WILLIAM GLACKENS (1870–1938)
Luxembourg Gardens, 1906
Oil on canvas
23 ¾ x 32
Museum Purchase, William A. Clark Fund 37.1

HENRY McFEE (1886–1953)
Corner of a Room, c. 1935
Oil on canvas
40 x 30
Museum Purchase, William A. Clark Fund 37.2

WELLS SAWYER (1863–1961)
Winter at Snug Rock, before 1936
Oil on composition board
16 ¼ x 20 ¼
Gift of the Friends of the Artist 40.20

ALEXANDER BROOK
Peggy Bacon (formerly *My Wife*), 1932

GEORGE LUKS
Woman with Black Cat, 1932

THE SIXTEENTH BIENNIAL EXHIBITION OF CONTEMPORARY AMERICAN OIL PAINTINGS
March 26 – May 7, 1939

ROBERT PHILIPP (1895–1981)
Nude, 1933
Oil on canvas
41 x 29 ⅝
Museum Purchase, William A. Clark Fund 39.4
Second William A. Clark Prize and
Corcoran Silver Medal

ALBERT SERWAZI (1905–1992)
Model Resting, 1938–39
Oil on canvas
22 ¼ x 27 ¼
Fourth Honorable Mention
Gift of the Artist 1974.79

FRANKLIN CHENAULT WATKINS (1894–1972)
Summer Fragrance, 1938
Oil on canvas
39 x 50 ¾
Museum Purchase, William A. Clark Fund 39.3
First William A. Clark Prize and Corcoran
Gold Medal

ANDREA DE ZEREGA (B. 1917)
Life Class, Monday Morning, 1936–37
Oil on canvas
36 ¼ x 44 ⅛
Gift of the Artist 67.31

THE SEVENTEENTH BIENNIAL EXHIBITION OF CONTEMPORARY AMERICAN OIL PAINTINGS
March 23 – May 4, 1941

JOHN HELIKER (B.1909)
Vermont Farm, 1940
Oil on canvas
16 x 20 ⅛
Museum Purchase, William A. Clark Fund 41.86
First William A. Clark Prize and Corcoran
Gold Medal

THE EIGHTEENTH BIENNIAL EXHIBITION OF CONTEMPORARY AMERICAN OIL PAINTINGS
March 21 – May 2, 1943

AARON BOHROD (1907–1992)
Wilmington Evening, 1942
Oil on gesso panel
24 x 32
Museum Purchase, William A. Clark Fund 43.3
Second William A. Clark Prize and Corcoran
Silver Medal

EDWARD HOPPER (1882–1967)
Ground Swell, 1939
Oil on canvas
36 ½ x 50 ³⁄₁₆
Museum Purchase, William A. Clark Fund 43.6

PEPPINO MANGRAVITE
Family Portrait, 1930

JEROME MYERS
Life on the East Side, 1931

ROSS MOFFETT
Provincetown Wharf, c. 1935

RICHARD LAHEY (1893–1978)
Carlotta, 1943
Oil on canvas
32 ⅜ x 32 ¼
Museum Purchase, Anna E. Clark Fund 43.7

HENRY MATTSON (1887–1971)
Rocks, 1942
Oil on canvas
32 ¼ x 42
Museum Purchase, William A. Clark Fund 43.2
First William A. Clark Prize and Corcoran Gold Medal

HOBART NICHOLS (1869–1962)
Sub-Zero, before 1943
Oil on canvas
30 x 35 ⅞
Gift of Archer M. Huntington 47.2

GEORGE PICKEN (1898–1971)
Convoy, 1942–43
Oil on canvas
15 ⅝ x 40 ⅛
Museum Purchase, William A. Clark Fund 43.5
Fourth William A. Clark Prize and Corcoran Honorable Mention
Certificate

ABRAM POOLE (1882–1961)
Kitty, c. 1939
Oil on canvas
40 ⅜ x 26 ⅜
Gift of Mrs. Paul B. Magnuson 62.19

RAPHAEL SOYER (1899–1988)
Waiting Room, c. 1940
Oil on canvas
34 x 45
Museum Purchase, William A. Clark Fund 43.4
Third William A. Clark Prize and Corcoran Bronze Medal

EUGEN WEISZ (1890–1954)
Still Life, 1943
Oil on canvas
20 ½ x 26
Museum Purchase, Anna E. Clark Fund 43.8
Returned to artist in 1943 as partial payment for *Self Portrait*
(14th Exhibition)

**THE NINETEENTH BIENNIAL EXHIBITION OF
CONTEMPORARY AMERICAN OIL PAINTINGS**
March 18 – April 29, 1945

ISABEL BISHOP (1902–1988)
Two Girls Outdoors, 1944
Oil on composition board
30 x 18 ⅛
Museum Purchase, Anna E. Clark Fund 45.6
Third William A. Clark Prize and Corcoran Bronze Medal

LEE JACKSON (B. 1909)
Fall Practice, 1943
Oil on composition board
15 x 22
Museum Purchase, Anna E. Clark Fund 45.7

Eugen Weisz
Self-Portrait, 1935

Henry McFee
Corner of a Room, c. 1935

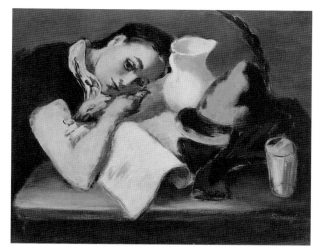

Albert Serwazi
Model Resting, 1938–39

Charles Locke (1899–1983)
Third Avenue El, 1943
Oil on canvas board
12 x 16
Museum Purchase, Anna E. Clark Fund 45.8

Alfred McAdams (b.1914)
By the Window (Portrait of June), 1945
Oil on masonite
36 x 26
Promised gift of the artist

Harold Weston (1894–1972)
Fruit Bowl, 1927–31
Oil on canvas
24 x 18 ½
Gift of Duncan Phillips 56.31

**Zsissly (Malvin Marr Albright)
(b.1897)**
Deer Island, Maine, 1940
Oil on canvas
28 ¼ x 62 ¼
Second William A. Clark Prize and
Corcoran Silver Medal
Museum Purchase, Anna E. Clark Fund 45.5

**The Twentieth Biennial Exhibition
of Contemporary American Oil
Paintings**
March 30 – May 11, 1947

Walter Stuempfig (1914–1970)
Two Houses, 1946
Oil on canvas
24 ⅞ x 30 ⅛
Museum Purchase, William A. Clark Fund 47.11
Second William A. Clark Prize and Corcoran
Silver Medal

**The Twenty-first Biennial
Exhibition of Contemporary
American Oil Paintings**
March 27 – May 8, 1949

Nicolai Cikovsky (1894–1984)
Spring Melody, 1948
Oil on canvas
42 x 31 ¾
Museum Purchase, William A. Clark Fund 49.21
Third Honorable Mention

Fred Conway (b. 1900)
Witchery, 1948
Encaustic on composition board
37 ¼ x 32 ¼
Museum Purchase, William A. Clark Fund 49.19
Second William A. Clark Prize and Corcoran
Silver Medal

Eric Isenburger (1902–1988)
Romantic Figure, 1948
Oil on canvas
50 x 40
Museum Purchase, Anna E. Clark Fund 49.18
First William A. Clark Prize and Corcoran Gold
Medal

Martin Jackson (b. 1919)
Harbor in the Night, 1948
Oil on canvas
24 ⅞ x 32
Museum Purchase, Anna E. Clark Fund 49.22
Fifth Honorable Mention

AARON BOHROD
Wilmington Evening, 1942

RAPHAEL SOYER
Waiting Room, c. 1940

HENRY MATTSON
Rocks, 1942

BROR JULIUS NORDFELDT (1878–1955)
Flood, 1948
Oil on canvas
40 x 52
Museum Purchase, William A. Clark Fund 49.20
Third William A. Clark Prize and Corcoran Bronze Medal

THE TWENTY-SECOND BIENNIAL EXHIBITION OF CONTEMPORARY AMERICAN OIL PAINTINGS
April 1 – May 13, 1951

SAMUEL BOOKATZ (B.1910)
Night Glow, 1951
Oil on canvas
59 ⅝ x 96 ⅝
Promised gift of the artist

PHILIP EVERGOOD (1901–1973)
Sunny Side of the Street, 1950
Egg-oil-varnish emulsion with marble dust and glass on canvas
50 x 36 ⅛
Museum Purchase, Anna E. Clark Fund 51.17
Second William A. Clark Prize and Corcoran Silver Medal

RICHARD HAINES (1906–1984)
Prodigal Son, 1949
Oil on canvas
30 x 40
Museum Purchase, Anna E. Clark Fund 51.18
Third William A. Clark Prize and Corcoran Bronze Medal

MARJORIE PHILLIPS (1894–1985)
Counterpoint, 1950
Oil on canvas
25 x 34
Gift of Marjorie Phillips with aid of funds from the Women's Committee
of the Corcoran Gallery of Art

HOBART NICHOLS
Sub-Zero, before 1943

CHARLES LOCKE
Third Avenue El, 1943

ISABEL BISHOP
Two Girls Outdoors, 1944

RAPHAEL SOYER (1899–1988)
Waiting for the Audition, 1950
Oil on canvas
30 x 24 ¼
Museum Purchase, William A. Clark Fund 51.16
First William A. Clark Prize and
Corcoran Gold Medal

**THE TWENTY-THIRD BIENNIAL
EXHIBITION OF CONTEMPORARY
AMERICAN OIL PAINTINGS**
March 15 – May 3, 1953

HOBSON PITTMAN (1900–1972)
Veiled Bouquet, 1950–51
Oil on canvas
29 ½ x 24 ½
Museum Purchase, Anna E. Clark Fund 53.3
Second William A. Clark Prize and Corcoran
Silver Medal

NICHOLAS VASILIEFF (1892–1970)
Pink Table Cloth, c. 1950
Oil on canvas
28 ½ x 42
Anonymous Gift 57.1

**THE TWENTY-FOURTH BIENNIAL
EXHIBITION OF CONTEMPORARY
AMERICAN OIL PAINTINGS**
March 13 – May 8, 1955

JOHN HULTBERG (B. 1922)
Yellow Sky, 1953
Oil on canvas
43 ¹³/₁₆ x 84
Museum Purchase, William A. Clark Fund 55.17
First William A. Clark Prize and Corcoran
Gold Medal

HENRY NIESE (B. 1924)
The Window, before 1955
Oil on composition board
36 x 28
Museum Purchase 55.19
Fourth William A. Clark Prize and
Corcoran Copper Medal (replaces Corcoran
Honorable Mention Certificate)

LARRY RIVERS (B. 1923)
Self-Figure, 1955
Oil on canvas
93 ⅜ x 65 ¼
Museum Purchase, William A. Clark Fund 55.18
Third William A. Clark Prize and Corcoran
Bronze Medal

THEODOROS STAMOS (1922–1997)
Heart of Norway Spruce, 1952
Oil on canvas
75 ⅛ x 12 ¹³/₁₆
Museum Purchase, Anna E. Clark Fund
and gift of anonymous donor 55.1

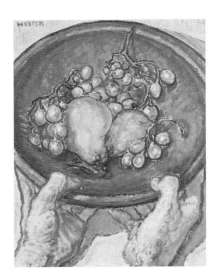

HAROLD WESTON
Fruit Bowl, 1927–31

NICOLAI CIKOVSKY
Spring Melody, 1948

ERIC ISENBURGER
Romantic Figure, 1948

ALFRED MC ADAMS
By the Window (Portrait of June), 1944

THE TWENTY-FIFTH BIENNIAL EXHIBITION OF CONTEMPORARY AMERICAN OIL PAINTINGS
January 13 – March 10, 1957

JOSEF ALBERS (1888–1976)
Homage to the Square: "Yes", 1956
Casein on masonite
39 ⅞ x 39 ⅞
Museum Purchase, William A. Clark Fund
57.8
Third William A. Clark Prize and Corcoran
Bronze Medal

LOREN MACIVER (B. 1909)
The Street, 1956
Oil on canvas
24 ¾ x 81
Museum Purchase, William A. Clark Fund
57.7
First William A. Clark Prize and Corcoran
Gold Medal

THE TWENTY-SIXTH BIENNIAL EXHIBITION OF CONTEMPORARY AMERICAN PAINTING
January 17 – March 8, 1959

LETA HESS (B. 1911)
Still Life, c. 1958
Oil on masonite
48 x 48
Museum Purchase, William A. Clark Fund
58.36
Fourth William A. Clark Prize and Corcoran
Copper Medal

MAX KAHN (B. 1904)
We Gather Together, c. 1958
Oil on canvas
32 x 42
Museum Purchase, William A. Clark Fund
58.35
Third William A. Clark Prize and Corcoran
Bronze Medal

YORAM KANIUK (B. 1929)
Dancer, 1953–54
Oil on canvas
50 x 40
Gift of Mr. and Mrs. Fred L. Palmer 58.25

WALTER PLATE (1925–1972)
Hot House, 1958
Oil on masonite
72 x 96
Museum Purchase, William A. Clark Fund
58.34
First William A. Clark Prize and Corcoran
Gold Medal

NICHOLAS VASILIEFF (1892–1970)
Portrait of Mrs V. (Woman in Red), 1956
Oil on canvas
47 ½ x 36
Gift of W. Montgomery Jackson 58.24

WALTER STUEMPFIG
Two Houses, 1946

BROR JULIUS NORDFELDT
Flood, 1948

THE TWENTY-SEVENTH BIENNIAL EXHIBITION OF CONTEMPORARY AMERICAN PAINTING
January 14 – February 28, 1961

WILL BARNET (B. 1911)
Multiple Images I, 1959
Oil on canvas
62 ³/₁₆ x 48 ³/₁₆
Museum Purchase, Anna E. Clark Fund 60.39
Third William A. Clark Prize and Corcoran
Bronze Medal

SIDNEY GROSS (1921–1969)
Untitled No. 6, 1960
Oil on canvas
66 ¼ x 84 ⅛
Gift of Mrs. Ruth M. Berstein 61.15

CHARLES SHAW (1892–1974)
Night Attack, 1960
Oil on canvas
50 ¼ x 75
Anonymous gift 61.23

THE TWENTY-EIGHTH BIENNIAL EXHIBITION OF CONTEMPORARY AMERICAN PAINTING
January 18 – March 3, 1963

LEE BONTECOU (B. 1931)
Untitled (57), 1961
Welded metal and painted canvas
46 x 70
Gift of the Ford Foundation 62.31
Second William A. Clark Prize and the Corcoran
Silver Medal

MARJOREE DEO (B.1907)
Foliage, 1962
Oil on masonite
48 x 40 ⅛
Museum Purchase 63.10

BURGOYNE DILLER (1906–1965)
First Theme, c. 1962
Oil on canvas
95 ¾ x 38
Gift of the Ford Foundation 62.32

JIMMY ERNST (1920–1984)
Icarus, 1962
Oil on canvas
55 ¼ x 76 ⅛
Gift of the Ford Foundation 62.33

ROBERT GOODNOUGH (B. 1917)
Figure Group: Abduction, 1960
Oil on canvas
58 x 68 ¼
Gift of the Ford Foundation 62.34

ROBERT HARVEY (B. 1924)
Norah, 1962
Oil on canvas
47 ¾ x 42
Gift of the Ford Foundation 62.35
Honorable Mention

RICO LEBRUN (1900–1964)
Night Figures #2, 1961
Oil on canvas
78 ¾ x 108 ⅝
Gift of the Friends of the Corcoran Gallery of Art
63.1

SAMUEL BOOKATZ
Night Glow, 1951

HOBSON PITTMAN
Veiled Bouquet, 1950–51

TEIJI TAKAI (B. 1911)
Aka, 1962
Oil on canvas
82 ½ x 70
Gift of Mrs. Leslie Randall 62.29

**THE TWENTY-NINTH BIENNIAL
EXHIBITION OF CONTEMPORARY
AMERICAN PAINTING**
February 26 – April 18, 1965

RICHARD ANUSZKIEWICZ (B. 1930)
Squaring the Circle, 1963
Oil on canvas
84 x 84
Gift of Dr. and Mrs. Julius S. Piver in memory of Mr.
and Mrs. Harry Piver through the Friends of the
Corcoran 64.30

GENE DAVIS (1920–1985)
Legato in Red
Acrylic on unsized canvas
124 x 224
Museum Purchase, Gallery Fund 65.2
Third William A. Clark Prize and
Corcoran Bronze Medal
Returned to artist in 1965 in exchange for *Blueprint
for Riveters*, which was exchanged for *Black Popcorn*
(30th exhibition)

STANLEY EDWARDS (B. 1941)
Infant on Altar, 1964
Oil on canvas
72 x 84
Gift of the Friends of Corcoran Gallery of Art 65.3

SUE FULLER (B. 1914)
String Composition #144, 1967
Nylon threads under Plexiglass
32 ½ x 32 ½
Gift of Mr. Emerson Crocker 68.18

STEPHEN GREENE (B. 1918)
The Watchers, 1962
Oil on canvas
50 x 68
Gift of Mr. and Mrs. David Lloyd Kreeger 65.4
Fourth William A. Clark Prize and Corcoran
Copper Medal

ALEXANDER LIBERMAN (B. 1912)
From Black to White, 1964
Acrylic on canvas
111 ½ x 236
Gift of the Artist 1969.10

HENRY PEARSON (B. 1914)
Number 27 – 1963, 1963
Oil on canvas
52 x 71
Gift of Mr. and Mrs. David Lloyd Kreeger 65.5

RICHARD POUSETTE-DART (1916–1992)
Ramapo Sky, 1963
Oil on canvas
50 ¾ x 75 ½
Gift of the Friends of the Corcoran Gallery of Art
65.6
Second William A. Clark Prize and Corcoran
Silver Medal

**THE THIRTIETH BIENNIAL
EXHIBITION OF CONTEMPORARY
AMERICAN PAINTING**
February 24 – April 19, 1967

GENE DAVIS (1920–1985)
Black Popcorn, 1965
Oil on canvas
114 x 114
Museum Purchase and exchange 67.7

John Hultberg
Yellow Sky, 1953

Nicholas Vasilieff
Portrait of Mrs V. (Woman in Red), 1956

Peter Golfinopoulos (b. 1928)
Homage to Joyce II, 1966
Oil on canvas
84 x 144
Gift of Josephine Cockrell Thornton 1991.43

Paul Jenkins (b. 1923)
Phenomena, Chosen Cycle, 1965
Acrylic on canvas
94 ½ x 51
Gift of David Klugar 67.5

Paul Jenkins (b. 1923)
Day of Zagorsk, 1966
Acrylic on canvas
60 x 114
Gift of the Artist 67.10

Jules Olitski (b. 1922)
Pink Alert, 1966
Acrylic on canvas
113 x 80
Gift of the Friends of the Corcoran Gallery
of Art 67.12
First William A. Clark Prize and
Corcoran Gold Medal

**The Thirty-first Biennial
Exhibition**
February 1 – March 16, 1969

Dean Fleming (b. 1933)
Atlantis, 1967
Enamel on nine masonite panels
108 x 132
Museum Purchase, Mr. and Mrs. David
Lloyd Kreeger Purchase Award 1969.35

Michael Goldberg (b. 1924)
Untitled, 1968
Oil and pastel
48 x 48
Museum Purchase, Director's Discretionary
Fund 1969.20

Irene Rice Pereira (1907–1971)
*The Circumnavigation of the Sphering
of the Poles,* 1964
Oil on canvas
56 x 50
Gift of the Associates of the Corcoran
Gallery of Art 1969.24

Robert Swain (b. 1940)
Untitled, No 7, 1968–69
Acrylic on canvas
153 x 306
Gift of Mary Howland Chase and the
Friends of the Corcoran Gallery of Art
1969.13

Richard Tuttle (b. 1941)
Red Canvas, 1967
Dyed canvas
57 x 55
Gift of Mr. Eric Green 1969.38

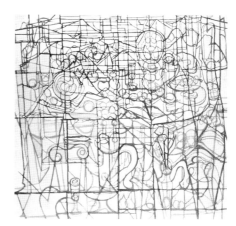

Leta Hess
Still Life, c. 1958

RICHARD ANUSZKIEWICZ
Squaring the Circle, 1963

ROBERT GOODNOUGH
Figure Group: Abduction, 1960

120

THE THIRTY-SECOND BIENNIAL EXHIBITION OF CONTEMPORARY AMERICAN PAINTING
February 28 – April 4, 1971

EDWARD MOSES (B. 1926)
Teec, 1970
Acrylic resin and powdered pigment
on canvas
88 x 111
Gift of the Women's Committee of the Corcoran
Gallery of Art 1971.14

FRANKLIN OWEN (B. 1939)
Mandan, No. 19, 1970
Acrylic on canvas
78 x 124
Gift of the Friends of the Corcoran Gallery of Art
1971.7.1

PHILIP PEARLSTEIN (B. 1924)
Reclining Nude on Green Couch, 1971
Oil on canvas
60 x 48
Gift of the Friends of the Corcoran Gallery of Art
1971.7.2
Courtesy of Robert Miller Gallery, New York

THE THIRTY-THIRD BIENNIAL EXHIBITION OF CONTEMPORARY AMERICAN PAINTING: THE WAY OF COLOR
February 24 – April 8, 1973

MORTEZA SAZEGAR (B. 1933)
C5-72 #1, 1972
Acrylic on canvas
72 x 72
Gift of Mr. and Mrs. Gilbert H. Kinney 1974.69

THE THIRTY-FOURTH BIENNIAL EXHIBITION OF CONTEMPORARY AMERICAN PAINTING
February 22 – April 6, 1975

RONALD DAVIS (B. 1937)
T Beam, 1974
Acrylic and dry pigment on canvas
111 ½ x 144
Gift of the Friends of the Corcoran Gallery of Art
1975.8

JOAN SNYDER (B. 1940)
Creek Square, 1974
Oil, acrylic, canvas, cheesecloth, papier mâché
on canvas
60 ¼ x 60 ¼
Gift of Marvin and Florence Gerstin 1985.14

RICO LEBRUN
Night Figures #2, 1961

JIMMY ERNST
Icarus, 1962

RICHARD POUSETTE-DART
Ramapo Sky, 1963

THE THIRTY-FIFTH BIENNIAL EXHIBITION OF CONTEMPORARY AMERICAN PAINTING
February 26 – April 3, 1977

MICHAEL CLARK (B. 1946)
San Francisco Chinatown Window, 1976
Oil on linen
30 x 36
Gift of the Friends of the Corcoran Gallery of Art
1977.11

FREDERICK HAMMERSLEY (B. 1919)
Refer Two, 1973–74
Oil on linen
42 x 42
Museum Purchase, William A. Clark Fund 1977.5

SANDI SLONE (B. 1939)
Shivernly, 1976
Acrylic on canvas
81 x 69
Gift of Bruce L. Ehrmann 1998.10

THE THIRTY-SIXTH BIENNIAL EXHIBITION OF CONTEMPORARY AMERICAN PAINTING
February 24 – April 8, 1979
No Acquisitions

THE THIRTY-SEVENTH BIENNIAL EXHIBITION OF CONTEMPORARY AMERICAN PAINTING
February 19 – April 5, 1981

JOAN MITCHELL (1926–1992)
Salut Tom, 1979
Oil on canvas
110 $^{7}/_{16}$ x 314 ½
Musuem Purchase with aid of funds from the
Women's Committee of the Corcoran Gallery of Art
and the National Endowment for the Arts, 1979.18

THE THIRTY-EIGHTH BIENNIAL EXHIBITION OF CONTEMPORARY AMERICAN PAINTING/SECOND WESTERN STATES EXHIBITION
February 3 – April 3, 1983
No Acquisitions

THE THIRTY-NINTH BIENNIAL EXHIBITION OF CONTEMPORARY AMERICAN PAINTING
February 2 – April 7, 1985
No Acquisitions

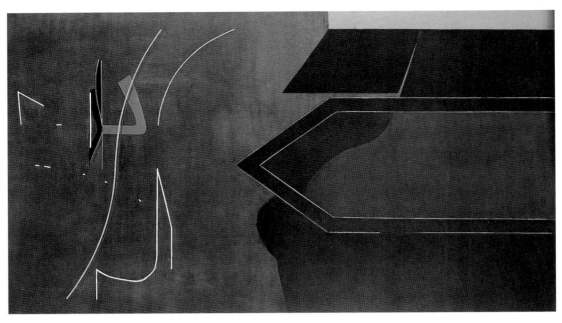

PETER GOLFINOPOULOS
Homage to Joyce II, 1966

THE FORTIETH BIENNIAL
EXHIBITION OF CONTEMPORARY
AMERICAN PAINTING
April 11 – June 21, 1987

MARY HEILMANN (B. 1940)
The Beach House, 1986
Oil on canvas
60 x 42
Gift of the Friends of the Corcoran Gallery of Art
1987.9.1

ROBERT MANGOLD (B. 1937)
Five Color Frame Painting, 1985
Acrylic on canvas
94 ¾ x 78 ½
Gift of the Women's Committee of the Corcoran
Gallery of Art 1987.10

HARVEY QUAYTMAN (B. 1937)
Age of Iron, 1986
Acrylic, rust, and collage on canvas
39 ⅞ x 39 ⅞
Gift of the Friends of the Corcoran Gallery of Art
1987.9.2

SEAN SCULLY (B. 1945)
Flyer, 1986
Oil on canvas
102 ¼ x 119
Gift of the Women's Committee of the Corcoran
Gallery of Art in memory of Jinx Cutts with aid of
funds from the Firestone Foundation and the Jinx
Cutts Memorial Fund 1986.8

THE FORTY-FIRST BIENNIAL
EXHIBITION OF CONTEMPORARY
AMERICAN PAINTING
April 5 – June 4, 1989
No Acquisitions

THE FORTY-SECOND BIENNIAL
EXHIBITION OF CONTEMPORARY
AMERICAN PAINTING
September 7 – November 10, 1991

L. C. ARMSTRONG (B. 1954)
Re-Coil, 1990
Enamel, fuse burn and resin on three steel panels
60 x 108
Gift of the Women's Committee of the
Corcoran Gallery of Art 1991.40.1

LYDIA DONA (B. 1955)
*Fear of Falling into the Lack, The Dream of
Language, and the Ruptures of the Flood*, 1991
Oil, acrylic and sign paint on canvas
84 ¼ x 64
Gift of the Women's Committee of the
Corcoran Gallery of Art 1991.40.2

WILLY HEEKS (B. 1951)
Solace, 1990
Oil and charcoal on canvas
90 x 106
Gift of the Friends of the Corcoran Gallery of Art
1991.15.2

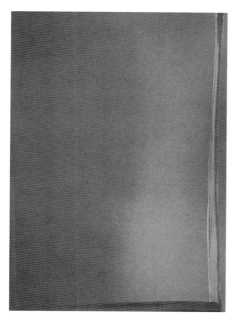

JULES OLITSKI
Pink Alert, 1966

LARI PITTMAN (B. 1952)
Reverential and Needy, 1991
Acrylic and enamel on mahogany panel
65 x 82
Gift of the Friends of the Corcoran Gallery of Art
1992.1

THOMAS ERIC STANTON (B. 1947)
Tree of Life (Hannibal), 1991
Mixed media on canvas
118 x 88
Museum Purchase, William A. Clark Fund 1991.50

**THE FORTY-THIRD BIENNIAL
EXHIBITION OF CONTEMPORARY
AMERICAN PAINTING**
October 30, 1993 – January 2, 1994

IDA APPLEBROOG (B. 1929)
Mother mother I am ill, 1993
Oil on canvas
110 x 72
Museum Purchase, the Jacob and Charlotte Lehrman
Foundation Memorial Art Fund 1998.19

KIM DINGLE (B. 1951)
Black Girl Dragging White Girl, 1992
Oil and charcoal on canvas
72 x 60
Gift of the Women's Committee of the Corcoran
Gallery of Art 1993.1.1

CHARLES GARABEDIAN (B. 1923)
Study for "The Iliad", 1992
Acrylic on paper
43 ⅜ x 80
Gift of the Friends of the Corcoran Gallery of Art
1994.3.1

**THE FORTY-FOURTH BIENNIAL
EXHIBITION OF CONTEMPORARY
AMERICAN PAINTING: PAINTING
OUTSIDE PAINTING**
December 16, 1995 – February 19, 1996

STUART ARENDS (B. 1950)
O.S. 50, 1994
Oil on steel
4 ½ x 3 ¾ x 3 ¾
Gift of the Artist 1996.7

FABIAN MARCACCIO (B. 1963)
Paint-Zone #12, 1994–5
Collograph, oil on canvas
66 x 60
Promised gift of Anthony T. Podesta

JESSICA STOCKHOLDER (B. 1959)
1994, 1994
Plastic sink legs, clothing, trimming, string, yarn,
wood, hardware, piece of furniture, papier mâché,
plaster, wallpaper paste, glue, and plastic fruit
93 x 50 x 82
Gift of the Women's Committee of the Corcoran
Gallery of Art 1996.2.1

Index to the Checklist

Abbey, Edwin Austin (1852–1911) *1st Biennial*

Albers, Josef (1888–1976) *25th Biennial*

Albright, Malvin Marr, see Zsissly

Anshutz, Thomas (1851–1912) *1st Biennial*

Anuszkiewicz, Richard (b. 1930) *29th Biennial*

Applebroog, Ida (b. 1929) *43rd Biennial*

Arends, Stuart (b. 1950) *44th Biennial*

Armstrong, L. C. (b. 1954) *42nd Biennial*

Baker, Samuel Burtis (1882–1967) *8th Biennial*

Barnet, Will (b. 1911) *27th Biennial*

Bartlett, Frederic (1873–1953) *7th Biennial*

Beaux, Cecilia (1863–1942) *9th Biennial*

Benson, Frank Weston (1862–1951) *4th, 7th, 10th Biennials*

Betts, Louis (1873–1961) *9th Biennial*

Biddle, George (1885–1973) *15th Biennial*

Bishop, Isabel (1902–1988) *19th Biennial*

Blakelock, Ralph Albert (1847–1919) *1st Biennial*

Bloch, Julius (1888–1966) *14th Biennial*

Bogert, George (1864–1944) *1st Biennial*

Bohrod, Aaron (1907-1922) *18th Biennial*

Bontecou, Lee (b. 1931) *28th Biennial*

Bookatz, Samuel (b. 1910) *22nd Biennial*

Brook, Alexander (1898–1980) *13th Biennial*

Brooke, Richard Norris (1847–1920) *4th Biennial*

Burroughs, Bryson (1869–1934) *12th Biennial*

Carlsen, Dines (1901–1966) *6th Biennial*

Carlsen, Emil (1853–1932) *6th, 8th, 10th Biennials*

Carlson, John Fabian (1875–1945) *4th Biennial*

Cassatt, Mary Stevenson (1844–1926) *1st, 2nd Biennials*

Chase, William Merritt (1849–1916) *6th Biennial*

Cikovsky, Nicolai (1894–1984) *21st Biennial*

Clark, Michael (b. 1946) *35th Biennial*

Conner, John (1869–1945) *14th Biennial*

Conway, Fred (b. 1900) *21st Biennial*

Crane, Bruce (1857–1937) *5th Biennial*

Critcher, Catharine (1876–1968) *9th Biennial*

Davey, Randall (1887–1964) *14th Biennial*

Davies, Arthur Bowen (1862–1928) *11th Biennial*

Davis, Gene (1920–1985) *29th, 30th Biennials*

Davis, Ronald (b. 1937) *34th Biennial*

DeCamp, Joseph Rodefer (1858–1923) *6th Biennial*

Deo, Marjoree (b.1907) *28th Biennial*

Dickinson, Sidney (1890–1978) *6th Biennial*

Diller, Burgoyne (1906–1965) *28th Biennial*

Dingle, Kim (b. 1951) *43rd Biennial*

Dona, Lydia (b. 1955) *42nd Biennial*

Dougherty, Paul (1877–1947) *1st Biennial*

Edwards, Stanley (b. 1941) *29th Biennial*

Ernst, Jimmy (1920–1984) *28th Biennial*

Evergood, Philip (1901–1973) *22nd Biennial*

Farley, Richard (1875–1954) *5th Biennial*

Fleming, Dean (b. 1933) *31st Biennial*

Folinsbee, John (1892–1972) *8th Biennial*

Ford, Lauren (1891–1981) *14th Biennial*

Foster, Ben (1852–1926) *3rd, 4th Biennials*

Frieseke, Frederick (1874–1939) *7th, 8th, 9th Biennials*

Fuller, Sue (b. 1914) *29th Biennial*

Garabedian, Charles (b. 1923) *43rd Biennial*

Garber, Daniel (1880–1958) *3rd, 8th, 11th Biennials*

Glackens, William (1870–1938) *15th Biennial*

Goldberg, Michael (b. 1924) *31st Biennial*

Golfinopoulos, Peter (b. 1928) *30th Biennial*

Goodnough, Robert (b. 1917) *28th Biennial*

Grabach, John (1886–1981) *12th Biennial*

Greene, Stephen (b. 1918) *29th Biennial*

Groll, Albert Lorey (1866–1952) *1st, 3rd Biennials*

GROSS, SIDNEY (1921-1969) *27th Biennial*

HAINES, RICHARD (1906-1984) *22nd Biennial*

HALE, LILLIAN WESTCOTT (1881-1963) *9th Biennial*

HALE, PHILIP (1865-1931) *5th Biennial*

HALLOWELL, GEORGE (1871-1926) *9th Biennial*

HAMMERSLEY, FREDERICK (B. 1919) *35th Biennial*

HARRISON, BIRGE (1854-1929) *5th Biennial*

HARVEY, ROBERT (B. 1924) *28th Biennial*

HASSAM, CHILDE (1859-1935) *1st, 4th, 7th Biennials*

HAWTHORNE, CHARLES (1872-1930) *9th Biennial*

HEEKS, WILLY (B. 1951) *42nd Biennial*

HEILMANN, MARY (B. 1940) *40th Biennial*

HELIKER, JOHN (B. 1909) *17th Biennial*

HENRI, ROBERT (1865-1929) *7th, 9th Biennials*

HESS, LETA (B. 1911) *26th Biennial*

HOMER, WINSLOW (1836-1910) *1st Biennial*

HOPPER, EDWARD (1882-1967) *18th Biennial*

HOWELL, FELICIE (1897-1968) *7th Biennial*

HULTBERG, JOHN (B. 1922) *24th Biennial*

ISENBURGER, ERIC (1902-1988) *21st Biennial*

JACKSON, LEE (B. 1909) *19th Biennial*

JACKSON, MARTIN (B. 1919) *21st Biennial*

JENKINS, PAUL (B. 1923) *30th Biennial*

JOHANSEN, JOHN (1876-1964) *9th, 10th Biennials*

KAHN, MAX (B. 1904) *26th Biennial*

KANIUK, YORAM (B. 1929) *26th Biennial*

KARFIOL, BERNARD (1886-1952) *11th Biennial*

KENDALL, WILLIAM (1869-1938) *2nd Biennial*

KENT, ROCKWELL (1882-1971) *13th Biennial*

LAHEY, RICHARD (1893-1978) *18th Biennial*

LAWSON, ERNEST (1873-1939) *6th Biennial*

LEBRUN, RICO (1900-1964) *28th Biennial*

LEVER, HAYLEY (1876-1958) *6th Biennial*

LIBERMAN, ALEXANDER (B. 1912) *29th Biennial*

LIE, JONAS (1880-1940) *11th Biennial*

LOCKE, CHARLES (1899-1983) *19th Biennial*

LOCKWOOD, WILTON (1861-1914) *1st Biennial*

LUKS, GEORGE (1867-1933) *13th Biennial*

MACCAMERON, ROBERT LEE (1866-1912) *2nd Biennial*

MACEWEN, WALTER (1860-1943) *2nd Biennial*

MACIVER, LOREN (B. 1909) *25th Biennial*

MANGOLD, ROBERT (B. 1937) *40th Biennial*

MANGRAVITE, PEPPINO (1896-1978) *13th Biennial*

MARCACCIO, FABIAN (B. 1963) *44th Biennial*

MATTSON, HENRY (1887-1971) *18th Biennial*

McADAMS, ALFRED (B. 1914) *19th Biennial*

McFEE, HENRY (1886-1953) *11th, 15th Biennials*

MELCHERS, GARI (1860-1932) *1st, 3rd, 5th Biennials*

METCALF, WILLARD LEROY (1858-1925) *1st Biennial*

MILLER, RICHARD (1875-1943) *14th Biennial*

MITCHELL, JOAN (1926-1992) *37th Biennial*

MOFFETT, ROSS (1888-1971) *14th Biennial*

MOSES, EDWARD (B. 1926) *32nd Biennial*

MURPHY, JOHN (1853-1921) *7th Biennial*

MYERS, JEROME (1867-1940) *13th Biennial*

NICHOLS, HOBART (1869-1962) *18th Biennial*

NIESE, HENRY (B. 1924) *24th Biennial*

NOBLE, JOHN (1874?-1934) *12th Biennial*

NORDFELDT, BROR JULIUS (1878-1955) *21st Biennial*

OCHTMAN, LEONARD (1854-1934) *2nd Biennial*

OLITSKI, JULES (B. 1922) *30th Biennial*

OWEN, FRANKLIN (B. 1939) *32nd Biennial*

PAXTON, WILLIAM (1869-1941) *6th Biennial*

PEARCE, CHARLES (1851-1914) *2nd Biennial*

PEARLSTEIN, PHILIP (B. 1924) *32nd Biennial*

PEARSON, HENRY (B. 1914) *29th Biennial*

PEREIRA, IRENE RICE (1907–1971) *31st Biennial*

PERRIE, BERTHA (1868–1921) *7th Biennial*

PHILIPP, ROBERT (1895–1981) *16th Biennial*

PHILLIPS, J. CAMPBELL (1873–1949) *5th Biennial*

PHILLIPS, MARJORIE (1894–1985) *22nd Biennial*

PICKEN, GEORGE (1898–1971) *18th Biennial*

PITTMAN, HOBSON (1900–1972) *23rd Biennial*

PITTMAN, LARI (B. 1952) *42nd Biennial*

PLATE, WALTER (1925–1972) *26th Biennial*

PLATT, CHARLES (1861–1933) *7th Biennial*

POOLE, ABRAM (1882–1961) *18th Biennial*

POUSETTE-DART, RICHARD (1916–1992) *29th Biennial*

PRENDERGAST, MAURICE (1859–1924) *9th Biennial*

QUAYTMAN, HARVEY (B. 1937) *40th Biennial*

REDFIELD, EDWARD (1869–1965) *1st, 5th, 8th, 9th Biennials*

REID, ROBERT (1862–1929) *2nd, 6th Biennials*

REIFFEL, CHARLES (1862–1942) *3rd Biennial*

RIVERS, LARRY (B. 1923) *24th Biennial*

ROOK, EDWARD (1870–1960) *7th Biennial*

RYDER, CHAUNCEY FOSTER (1868–1949) *4th Biennial*

SARGENT, JOHN SINGER (1856–1925) *5th, 6th Biennials*

SAWYER, WELLS (1863–1961) *15th Biennial*

SAZEGAR, MORTEZA (B. 1933) *33rd Biennial*

SCHOFIELD, ELMER (1867–1944) *2nd, 8th Biennials*

SCULLY, SEAN (B. 1945) *40th Biennial*

SERWAZI, ALBERT (1905–1992) *16th Biennial*

SEYFFERT, LEOPOLD (1887–1956) *9th, 10th Biennials*

SHANNON, JAMES JEBUSA (1862–1923) *1st Biennial*

SHAW, CHARLES (1892–1974) *27th Biennial*

SHURTLEFF, ROSWELL (1835–1915) *1st Biennial*

SILVETTE, DAVID (B. 1909) *13th Biennial*

SLOAN, JOHN (1871–1951) *13th Biennial*

SLONE, SANDI (B. 1939) *35th Biennial*

SMILLIE, JAMES DAVID (1833–1909) *1st Biennial*

SNYDER, JOAN (B. 1940) *34th Biennial*

SOYER, RAPHAEL (1899–1988) *18th, 22nd Biennials*

SPEICHER, EUGENE (1883–1962) *12th Biennial*

SPENCER, ROBERT (1879–1931) *7th Biennial*

STAMOS, THEODOROS (1922–1997) *24th Biennial*

STANTON, THOMAS ERIC (B. 1947) *42nd Biennial*

STERNE, MAURICE (1878–1957) *12th Biennial*

STOCKHOLDER, JESSICA (B. 1959) *44th Biennial*

STUEMPFIG, WALTER (1914–1970) *20th Biennial*

SWAIN, ROBERT (B. 1940) *31st Biennial*

SYMONS, GEORGE (1863–1930) *3rd, 7th Biennial*

TAKAI, TEIJI (B. 1911) *28th Biennial*

TARBELL, EDMUND CHARLES (1862–1938) *2nd, 6th Biennials*

THOMPSON, JOHN (1882–1945) *14th Biennial*

THORNE, WILLIAM (1864–1956) *1st Biennial*

TURNER, HELEN (1858–1958) *5th Biennial*

TUTTLE, RICHARD (B. 1941) *31st Biennial*

TYLER, HENRY (1855–1931) *9th Biennial*

UFER, WALTER (1876–1936) *8th, 9th Biennials*

VASILIEFF, NICHOLAS (1892–1970) *23rd, 26th Biennials*

VONNOH, ROBERT (1858–1933) *10th Biennial*

WALKER, HORATIO (1858–1938) *1st Biennial*

WATKINS, FRANKLIN CHENAULT (1894–1972) *16th Biennial*

WEIR, JULIAN ALDEN (1852–1919) *4th, 5th, 7th Biennials*

WEISZ, EUGEN (1890–1954) *14th, 18th Biennials*

WESTON, HAROLD (1894–1972) *19th Biennial*

WILES, IRVING RAMSAY (1861–1948) *3rd Biennial*

WOODBURY, CHARLES (1864–1940) *7th Biennial*

YOUNG, CHARLES (1869–1964) *6th Biennial*

ZEREGA, ANDREA DE (B. 1917) *16th Biennial*

ZSISSLY, (MALVIN MARR ALBRIGHT) (B. 1897) *19th Biennial*